PUT YOUR
FAITH
WHERE YOUR FORK IS

Science-Based, Faith-Empowered
Principles for Healthy Weight Management

Nettye Johnson

NJ PUBLISHING
DENHAM SPRINGS, LOUISIANA

Published by NJ Publishing

www.nettyejohnson.com

Requests for information should be addressed to info@nettyejohnson.com

For media or print interviews with Nettye Johnson, contact info@nettyejohnson.com

Printed in the United States of America

First Printing, 2016 Nettye Johnson/NJ Publishing

www.nettyejohnson.com

Quantity sales. Special discounts are available on quantity purchases by churches, associations, and others. For details, email the "Special Sales Department" at info@nettyejohnson.com.

Put Your Faith Where Your Fork Is/ Nettye Johnson. —1st ed.

ISBN 978-0692622216

Dedication

To all who refuse to live beneath their
God-given potential.

Contents

Acknowledgements

To God be the glory, honor, and praise.

To Will, my love, my friend, my Boaz.
Thank you for loving, leading, and encouraging me.

To Jabari and Etana, my blessing, my heritage, my legacy.
Thank you for making Momma's heart smile.

Disclaimer

This publication is designed to provide accurate and authoritative information with regard to the subject matter covered. The information and advice in this book are not intended to replace the services of a qualified medical professional. You are advised to consult with your healthcare professional with all matters relating to your health. You are also advised to seek the opinion of a medical professional before starting any diet, exercise, or other health program.

Bible Versions

Introduction

Beloved, I pray that you may prosper in all things and
be in health, just as your soul prospers.
3 John 2 (NKJV)

... apart from me you can do nothing.
John 15:5b

OUR NATION IS OUT of shape. The statistics do not lie.

- Sixty-nine percent of adults in this country are overweight or obese.[1]

- Chronic disease is the leading cause of death and disability, with one of every two adults affected.[2]

- Despite medical advances, for the first time in modern history, due to obesity, the life expectancy of children is shorter than preceding generations.[3]

We are increasingly sedentary, overfed, and undernourished. Millions are suffering and dying, and at the root of this problem is a serious case of fork and couch.

In the body of Christ, weight challenges loom larger. Studies indicate that:

- People who attend church are more likely to be 20 percent overweight and have higher blood pressure and cholesterol numbers than individuals who do not attend church.

- Seventy-six percent of pastors/clergy are overweight.

- Young adults who attend worship or Bible study once a week are 50 percent more likely to be obese.[4]

When it comes to the church and food, gluttony is an accepted and protected vice despite harmful health outcomes. The church is meant to be an active agent for help and healing. Our poor physical condition from poor physical stewardship limits this important work. A change must come.

Do you need a change?

Before you answer, consider more than the number on the scale. We are body, soul, and spirit. When the physical aspect of our triune nature is neglected, all areas of our existence suffer.

- Is your energy, health, or fitness less than it could be?

- When you look in your closet, is gratitude for the blessings right in front of you squelched by frustration at the shrinking percentage of clothing that fits?

- Do you feel trapped? Tied to medications, burdened with chronic illness, or caught up in harmful behaviors you can control—but don't?

- Have you invested a lot of time, energy, money, and worry in your weight, yet remain unable to reach or maintain your goal?

- Are you physically unable to walk the path, do the work, and fully enjoy the blessings God has planned for you?

- Does the condition of your body cause you to live beneath your purpose and potential?

If any of these statements ring true for you, beloved, take a deep breath. Hope and help are in this book.

My Journey

As a Bible teacher, certified health coach, and founder of a Christian wellness organization, I strive to help people grow in spiritual and physical stewardship. Faith-focused weight management is one of my areas of specialty.

I think it is important to note that I am not a former athlete or lifelong fit person telling others how to get in shape. Far from it. I know weight challenges well, having battled them myself for close to 30 years. Glory to God, the battle is done and won. My purpose is to help others along this path.

My healthy lifestyle was a long time coming. I was a socially introverted, academically focused child raised in a Mississippi-bred family transplanted to the Southside of Chicago. All my meals were good old, down-home, Southern soul food, served in abundance with love. I was also overweight and sedentary, and I suffered from exercise-induced asthma. At the time, I didn't think my weight and physical limitations fazed me. I wore the Pretty Plus line of clothing from Sears and focused on the Pretty part.

In high school, I failed PE. *(Hard to do.)* During the swimming unit, I was too ashamed to be seen in a bathing suit, so I stopped going to class. The limitations of my body (both real and exaggerated/imagined) limited my life.

In summer school PE, I spent several hours per day completing laps and attempting softball and volleyball. I passed the class, slimmed down, and, unfortunately, discovered how (over)exercising and (under)eating caused pounds to come off.

Diabetes and heart disease are all over my family tree, and during my sophomore year in college, my father died unexpectedly in his sleep from hypertension-related heart disease. I still find it difficult to express the impact. Young women need their fathers. A few years later, in my early twenties, I was diagnosed with a heart abnormality. At the time, I was overweight (again), with a restaurant- and fast food- based diet and a weekend warrior activity regimen. I'm slow on the uptake, and it takes me a while to catch on, but I realized that to live in good health, my lifestyle had to change. I was not sure how to make that happen.

The next 20 years were spent trying to figure that out. Many, many, many, many diets and exercise plans were enthusiastically started and soon abandoned. You name it—I joined it, got the t-shirt, and all the suggested success-boosting materials. Each time, I'd get off to a great start and then fall back into old habits. Each time, lost pounds came back—and brought their buddies. I developed gallbladder disease, and the surgeon speculated that yo-yo dieting was the cause. In my attempts to be healthy, fit, and fine, I was making myself sick.

In 1999, I set a turn-of-the-century goal to get it together and joined Weight Watchers ... for the fourth (or maybe fifth) time. Again, I got down to a healthy weight and was so excited that I started working for the company as a part-time leader. Shortly after that, I left my career in technology and progressed to corporate positions with Weight Watchers, delivering training across the nation and later managing business operations for the state of Texas. Over the next decade, I was blessed to observe and assist thousands on their path to change. Beyond the company's customers, I also watched the fitness, health, and wellness efforts of family, friends, and fellow church members. I saw many successes and many struggles, not only from those in the process of change, but also from those who had reached their goals.

Shoot, I continued to struggle. I had babies. Worked a lot. Worked out a lot. Stressed a lot. So I ate a lot. I was out of balance, often out of shape, and despite strong faith, good knowledge, and amazing resources, I struggled with weight and wellness. While I was seriously solid on what to do, I was super-shaky on doing it.

In 2010, I left the corporate world to be home with my children. By this time, I was weight-lossed out! I was sick and tired of talking, thinking, and worrying about my weight. Without the structure and resources, I'd counted on, I was prepared to sit down, pick up my fork, and let the pounds settle where they pleased.

But God desired more. In that surrendered place of sick and tired, God met me.

Things. Changed.

God Changed My Mind and Heart

The Holy Spirit led me to earnestly examine the alignment of my beliefs and actions. (Again, I'm slow on the uptake, so these challenges came over and over.) Here are just a few:

- As a woman of faith, how can I declare, *"So if the Son sets you free, you will be free indeed"* (John 8:36), yet live in bondage to a cookie, dish of peach cobbler, or fried catfish plate?

- As a child of the King, how can I affirm, *"I can do all things through Christ who strengthens me"* (Philippians 4:13 NKJV), then say I can't exercise consistently?

- As one who knows this body is not my own—it was bought with a price—a temple of the Holy Spirit (1 Corinthians 6:19-20), how can I know this to be true and yet consistently behave in a way that is harmful?

I thought I was tired of struggling with weight. In truth, I was tired of struggling with contradiction —knowing full well what God has called and equipped me to do to steward my body—and choosing not to do it.

> *I thought I was tired of struggling with weight. In truth, I was tired of struggling with contradiction.*

My wallowing and whining persisted.

But God, it's so hard!

God said, "Is anything too hard for me?" (Jeremiah 32:27)

But God, I can't do it!

God's Word shows What I cannot do, God will. (Genesis 41:15-16)

But God, You know I've tried a gazillion times and keep failing.

God cannot fail.

God is the master, creator, and sustainer of all things. He knit my body together in my mother's womb and knows everything about me, yet I realized, when it came to the care of my body, I kept Him on the periphery, consistently pleasing and appeasing my flesh and asking the Lord to fix the consequences. My heart was pulled to let God in. Instead of acting first then asking God to bless my mess, I heard and began to heed the call to seek Him first and allow the Holy Spirit to guide my choices.

Peace, power, and lasting progress came when I took the focus off me (my desires, my efforts, my challenges, my deficiencies) and put the focus on God.

God Changed the Way I View Food

I love to eat (and frequently ate too much of the wrong things). I took knowledge that the Lord allowed me to amass over 20 years and purposed to put my faith where my fork is. This led to a mindful exploration of food, to being able to see it as a gift from God for nourishment and enjoyment. I progressed from fast food junkie to a fit foodie and clean eating advocate, sharing the benefits of farm-to-table and whole-food eating with anyone who would listen.

God Changed My Outlook on Exercise

I did not love to exercise. The Lord moved me from exercising because I knew I should to honestly enjoying exercise and counting it a privilege to offer that time as an act of worship. I moved from sporadic exercise to a three-time marathoner, encouraging others to lace up and embrace walking or running as a spiritual and physical discipline.

Faith-focused steps became habits, and as a result, the weight came off and stayed off. Today, I'm a member of the National Weight Control Registry (NCWR), a study of 10,000 people who have succeeded at long-term weight loss and maintenance.[5]

God Made My Passion My Purpose

Convinced of my call to progress health and physical stewardship, I began in-depth education and training on nutrition, exercise physiology and psychology, special population support, program design, and behavior modification. I also became a certified health coach, engaging individual clients, community groups, and church congregations.

From this service, *The Struggle Is Real But Not Necessary* series was born. The book series partners weight management best practices with a faith-focused view. *Put Your Faith Where Your Fork Is* is the first of this series.

What to Expect from This Book

In this book, you will not find the definition of or recommendation for a specific nutrition or diet program. Why not? Because everyone is unique. We have different medical requirements, body compositions, and body chemistry, varied abilities, schedules, lifestyles, and preferences such that what works for one person may not be effective or sustainable for someone else. One plan or program does not fit all.

There are, however, overarching spiritual and scientific principles that can move anyone to better health and wellness. This book is an impactful and universal collection of such principles.

Here you will find valuable truths and perspectives that help you:

- Put God first and grow closer to Him in the pursuit of health and wellness.

- Right skewed relationships with food.

- Embrace moderation and eliminate food guilt.

- Create a personalized, effective, and livable food philosophy for healthy weight loss and maintenance.

- Change your view of healthy disciplines from a challenge, battle, or struggle to a privilege, joy, a part of who you are, and a way to honor God.

As you read, have your Bible, a highlighter, and a pen nearby. Highlight statements that shine truth on your limiting beliefs and harmful habits.

Throughout the book, you will find calls for prayerful self-examination and application on Praction Pages.

According to the Urban Dictionary, praction is short for practice-action. I offer my husband's definition: prayer-action. Here, praction is the powerful step where prayer directs and moves the believer to take action.

Use the Praction Pages in this book to journal your prayers, record what the Holy Spirit laid on your heart (what God said), and outline your plan to heed His direction (what you will do).

Be open and honest with God and yourself as you answer the questions and journal.

Take notes.

Pray.

Plan.

Take action.

Don't rush through the book. Create a margin for the Holy Spirit to work and allow these life-changing principles to take root. Be forewarned, some parts may be uncomfortable. To shrink your body, you have to stretch beyond your comfort zone. Change rarely comes without challenge.

I'm pulling for you and praying that God uses the words in this book as a catalyst for transformation in your life.

I'm excited about the change to come. Step into the potential that God has for you.

Are you ready? Let's get started.

RENEW
YOUR MIND

Diets Do Work

Do not be deceived: God cannot be mocked. A man reaps what he sows. [8]Whoever sows to please their flesh, from the flesh will reap destruction; whoever sows to please the Spirit, from the Spirit will reap eternal life.
Galatians 6:7-8

SOCIETY HAS A CONFLICTED, dramatic relationship with diets.

I liken it to the relationship with reality TV. We talk a good game about how unreal reality television is. We call it trash and go on and on about how horrible it is for our society and personal psyche. Yet we watch.

Dieting gets similar treatment. Folks dog dieting out. In my line of work, I hear it often.

"I don't diet! Diet is a four-letter word."

Correct, it is four letters ...

"I don't diet! The first three letters of diet spell 'die.' Who wants to die? I want to live, so I have a 'liveit.'"

Granted, I lean towards the corny, but this makes me chuckle.

In my very non-scientific survey, the most popular anti-diet statement is the unofficial slogan of a few of the leading diet companies and programs.

"This is not a diet! It's a lifestyle."

Folks say these statements all the time. Dieting folks. In the past, I've made these statements. It all sounds great and it would be great—if it were true.

For all the side eye and trash talk thrown at diets, one would think the diet industry would be fledging. According to Marketdata Enterprises, Inc., in 2014, the U.S. weight loss market raked in $59,800,000,000.00.[6] That's billions. With a "b."

If dieting is no man's land, then why do millions of people devote billions of dollars and untabulated amounts of time and energy on them? Over and over again. To continue to the same thing and expect different results is insanity.

We are not insane, but the time has come to embrace the truth and call a spade a spade. The truth sets us free, right?

Let's stop defaming and denying diet because:

1. **Diet is a part of every person's life.**

2. **Diets do work.**

Before you think I'm crazy, let's lay out a few definitions.

Diet (noun) is defined as a pattern of eating. Everyone has a diet. You do. I do. People who swear they don't—they do as well. The question is, is your diet intentional? One that nurtures health and supports and maintains your best body? Or—is your diet unintentional? One that hinders health and makes you fluffy?

In all of the denying of diets, the diet most people have is the latter, a diet influenced by culture and marketing influences, laziness and the call of the flesh. These influences are discussed later in the book. Left unchecked, they lead to fat and faltering health.

US Food Consumption (as a % of calories)

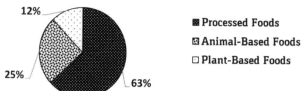

- ▨ Processed Foods
- ▨ Animal-Based Foods
- ▢ Plant-Based Foods

Source: USDA Economic Research Service, 2009; www.ers.usda.gov/publications/EIB33;
www.ers.usda.gov/Data/FoodGuideIndex.htm#calories
New York Coalition for Healthy School Food, www.healthyschoolfood.org

As a matter of fact, in this country, most people unknowingly but religiously follow what is called the Standard American Diet. The acronym for this pattern of eating says it all. It is SAD.

The bulk of our eating comes from processed foods. Fast and restaurant foods, boxed mixes, and frozen bagged items selected for convenience also include high amounts of added salt, fat, and sugar that add weight and harm health. The second-largest percentage of our nation's caloric intake comes from animal flesh and fat, about 25 percent. A small 12 percent of eating is from unprocessed plant-based fruits, vegetables, and grains. *Interestingly, ratios of many commercial weight loss programs can look like the SAD. They comprise very few whole, natural foods and lots of packaged meals, bars, snacks, smoothie mixes, etc., that are highly processed for reduced fat, reduced sugar, or reduced calories.*

We can and must choose better.

So, when we are fed up with the outcome of the default SAD diet, we buckle down and diet (verb).

To diet (verb) is to adopt a prescribed, regulated pattern of eating *for a period of time* for a specific purpose. Dieting has a place in certain circumstances, for example, an athlete preparing for an event or a person who needs surgery. The period of regulated eating would be in line to get their bodies ready for the upcoming event.

Here is the problem. Most people diet (verb) for a period of time. (Weight comes off.) They end the diet and go back to their SAD diet. (The weight comes back). Then comes all the "Diets don't work!" nonsense. If you have a pattern of repeat dieting, look back over your record. Does this ring true in your experience?

I believe, this is the fallacy of dieting. The temporary nature leads to temporary results. Most diets require a restrictive, non-livable pattern of eating and behavior for the length of the diet. Then some plans or programs tack on a short period of maintenance; that is a small fraction of the period time spent dieting. This is the setup for the fail. A new diet was not established because the bulk of the time, focus, and energy was devoted to a temporary set of behaviors.

Instead of dieting, I recommend you create a diet. Create a pattern of eating but don't plan to do it for just five weeks, five months, or even five years. Do not put a timeframe around the behaviors or choices with an anticipated release later. That does not work.

If you are hanging on and looking forward to the change that will happen at the end of the program or when you get to your goal—that's a good sign you are dieting!

For healthy weight maintenance, lose it like you will live it. This shift in mindset and action is free of weight loss and maintenance periods. From the jump, choose actions you enjoy and would be cool continuing for the rest of your life. This closes the door to rebound because every day is creating and substantiating habits—healthy habits that are congruent with a fit and healthy body. Do this and return to SAD, and the corresponding weight gain is less likely to occur.

Let's make this practical.

If you rely on counting calories, fat grams, carbs, or some kind of points to get the weight off, prepare to keep counting to keep the weight off.

If you rely on prepackaged foods or drinking shakes to get the weight off, be ready to keep opening packages or sipping to keep the weight off.

No shade on any programs that call for these measures—they do bring weight loss, and for a super-small number of people, they work for maintenance, too. Just make sure you count the cost before and prepare yourself for those actions to be your lifestyle.

Now, if you are like me, and the thought of counting or writing down everything you eat for the rest of your life sounds depressing, or you plan to chew food sometimes—don't rely on those methods to lose weight.

Use such methods for purposes other than weight maintenance. A few examples:

Maybe once a year if my eating gets shaky and I gain a few pounds, I do a restrictive cleanse or detox. Five to 12 pounds fall off depending on the length of the cleanse. The bulk of the loss is temporary. It would be foolish of me to believe otherwise. *I won't tell you how many times I embraced this thinking—and was disappointed.* That understood, I cleanse not for the loss of weight; I cleanse to flush my system, kill cravings, and reset to stable eating. The consistent healthy eating slowly reduces and stabilizes my weight back to my desired set point.

Another example: I often recommend that clients journal what they eat and drink for a short period of time. Research shows that food records are very effective in that they bring truth and awareness about our eating patterns. I encourage clients to use them as a tool for learning and then take the learning and put an appropriate change of eating in place. Rely on the change in eating that can be permanent. Do not rely on the process of tracking that is temporary.

Apply Galatians 6:7-8 to our body.

> *Do not be deceived: God cannot be mocked. A man reaps what he sows.* [8]*Whoever sows to please their flesh, from the flesh will reap destruction; whoever sows to please the Spirit, from the Spirit will reap eternal life.*

Refuse to be deceived. The truth of cause and effect applies to our body. We reap what we sow. Actions or circumstances cause weight to come on our body. Some action or circumstances continue to sustain the weight. The inverse also applies. Diets do work. Dieting does not.

Don't fall for the bait and switch that says do x (program) until you get to your goal, and then change to y for a bit and live it. Start with the y—an intentional diet that is healthy and fits your lifestyle and preferences. Let the Holy Spirit and the help or resources He enables (experience, scientific research, etc.) lead you to that diet. The next two chapters lay out scientific principles of fit and healthy eating to support this process.

Examine Thyself

One more point of reference. This is a critical foundation. Restore right positioning of God and food in your life.

Let God be God

Base all efforts in the knowledge that God loves you and cares about all of you. That includes the condition of your body.

In The Daniel Plan: 40 Days to a Healthier Life, Pastor Rick Warren states this understanding beautifully. Know and believe:

1. Your body belongs to God. (1 Corinthians 6:13)
2. Jesus paid for your body when He died for you on the cross. (1 Corinthians 6:19-20)
3. The Holy Spirit lives in your body. (1 Corinthians 6:19)
4. God expects you to take care of your body. This is physical stewardship.
5. God will resurrect your body after you die. (1 Corinthians 6:14)[7]

The scriptures for the references above are included at the end of this book for your convenience. Take a moment and reread the statements aloud, but this time, change the "you" and "your" to "me" and "mine." Make it personal.

God calls us to good physical stewardship. It honors Him and benefits us. He also equips us for the accomplishment of what He calls. Rest assured, beloved, you have all the resources you need to lose the weight and keep it off.

Devote the changes you make to lose weight and improve your health to God. This takes the focus off the end result of your goal and puts it on the steps of the journey. Do you only want to honor and please Him for a few weeks or until you get what you want to get out of it? Honor Him daily in the way you care for the temple of the Holy Spirit.

Let Food be Food

God is a jealous god (Exodus 20:3-5). We are commanded not to put any other god before Him. This includes food.

Prayerfully consider how you regard food. Do you feel out of control when it comes to food? Are you at the beck and call of your tastes? Do you turn to food when you are lonely, sad, stressed, or happy?

Has food taken a place of control or comfort that rightfully belongs to God?

If so, acknowledge it. Confess it. Renounce it and repent. Pray for the Holy Spirit to make you hyper-aware when you elevate food out of the place of a blessing from God to a god in your life.

Praction (Prayer - Action)

Journal your thoughts, prayer, and plan of action from this section.

CHAPTER 2

In Search of Healthy Weight

Do you know where you're goin' to?
Do you like the things that life is showin' you
Where are you goin' to? Do you know?
Theme from *Mahogany*
Gerry Goffin and Michael Masser

WEIGHT IS MORE THAN just the number on the scale. Simply defined, your weight is a measure of your body's mass, or how much gravity pulls on you. Before we go further, take this definition deeper. What else pulls on you as a result of the size and condition of your body?

Do you feel the pull of weight-related medical issues?

Does the pull of your body weight cause physical pain or discomfort?

Does your weight pull on your energy level or ability to accomplish what is before you?

Does your physical weight pull on you emotionally, affecting your self-image or self-esteem?

This book outlines principles to attain and sustain your healthy weight. This chapter and the next contain definitions of key terms and concepts related to weight loss. If these sections read like a textbook, my apologies. *For most, adipose tissue is not enthralling.* Dig in. These principles provide an important foundation.

Set Point Weight

A "set point" is a weight your body maintains with a small amount of fluctuation (about three to five pounds). This weight is natural for your body in that it tends to settle there without much effort.

Our bodies are highly adaptable, and they work to maintain a level of stability. Studies have shown that adults who don't try to control their weight up or down typically hover around a certain weight. Those of us who put a lot of effort into weight management are also probably familiar with weight set points. In the process of losing, with no change in the eating and exercise actions that were working like a charm, you hit a certain weight, and the scale refuses to budge. That place, also called a plateau, may be a set point for your body.

Here's a dose of reality. If, during the process of losing, you struggle (and I mean struggle) to get to a certain number on the scale, chances are, maintaining that number will be difficult. Set points are not struggle points. Struggle and stability are not compatible, and the body will gravitate to stability. (More on this in Chapter 3.)

In my quarter century of weight fluctuations, I've discovered four weight set points about 15 to 25 pounds from each other. These set points have become so familiar that I've given them names.

- **Plus 1 Weight.** This is my absolute max that requires another person (pregnancy weight).

- **Koo Koo Crazy Weight.** About 20 pounds below my max pregnancy weight is the weight my body holds when I eat as much I want, of what I want, whenever I want. Here my flesh leads. Truth be told, it is a miserable place. I'm sluggish and my blood pressure and cholesterol levels are borderline trouble. I feel swollen and uncomfortable in my skin.

- **Medically Healthy Weight.** About 20 to 25 pounds below my koo koo crazy weight is the place I settle after focused changes. Here I'm no longer medically classified as overweight, and my blood pressure and blood work are back in good ranges. Around this weight set point, I became a three-time marathoner and certified fitness instructor. I settle here in one of two ways: 1) When I pour time and energy into exercise but allow my eating to be shaky; or 2) when I focus on eating well but don't exercise consistently. The balance results in a place of comfort I called success for a long time. I thought it was the best my body could attain.

- **Healthy and Whole Weight.** Fifteen to 20 pounds below my medically healthy weight is my Healthy and Whole Weight. After a six-week fast (done for spiritual reasons), the Holy Spirit guided me to a balanced lifestyle of plant-based eating and moderate exercise where I live today. This place of ease and focus is the fittest and healthiest I have been in my adult life.

Genetics plays a part in set points. Lifestyle behaviors do as well. Genetics may dictate the maximums, minimums, and set points in between, but more dynamic elements influence at which set point the body settles. Things that can change (hormones, medications, eating habits, and exercise types and regularities) can affect where weight stabilizes.

If you are reading this book, I suppose your weight has settled at a place above where you want it to be. Give that set point a name.

I'm serious, give it a name!

Name it so you can tell it goodbye and remember you dismissed it when you notice the scale creeping back in that direction.

"Bye, _____"

Now welcome your new set point. Your healthy weight. This is exciting! Like a mother carrying a baby, you can name it now or name it when you arrive at that place. The choice is yours.

Named or not, take steps to begin to define that healthy weight.

Defining Your Healthy Weight

A healthy weight is often defined as a weight range at which an individual has reduced risk for chronic conditions and diseases.

Consider the top 10 causes of death in the United States in 2013:[8]

1. Heart disease
2. Cancer
3. Chronic lower respiratory diseases
4. Accidents (unintentional injuries)
5. Stroke (cerebrovascular diseases)
6. Alzheimer's disease
7. Diabetes
8. Influenza and pneumonia
9. Kidney diseases
10. Intentional self-harm (suicide)

Seven of the 10 are chronic diseases with weight-related factors. In its "Chronic Health Overview," the Centers for Disease Control and Prevention defines obesity as a "serious health concern." The overview states health risk behaviors: lack of physical activity, poor nutrition, tobacco use, and excess alcohol consumption "cause much of the illness, suffering, and early death related to chronic diseases and conditions."[9]

Health risk behaviors can be changed.

A few points of clarity.

Lower weight is not always a better weight. Too little body weight can be as harmful as excess body weight. There are plenty of thin people who are not healthy. The key is to find a weight range that benefits your health and well-being instead of limits it.

Your healthy weight is a place where medical, emotional, and spiritual elements are in agreement.

A healthy weight is not just medically defined. Your healthy weight has an emotional component—where you feel good about your weight and are comfortable in your skin. It also has a spiritual component—where your weight reflects good stewardship and enables you to live your purpose and potential. Don't discount any of these components. Your healthy weight is a place where medical, emotional, and spiritual elements are in agreement.

For the medical component, science provides multiple measures to help you zone in on your healthy weight.

BMI

Body mass index (BMI) replaces the height-weight tables established by insurance companies in the 1940s to gauge health risk. BMI calculations estimate body composition and reflect a correlation between body weight, disease, and death. To calculate your BMI, you will need your current weight and height. *Not the numbers on your driver's license. The truth sets us free!* Record those numbers below.

Weight _____ (lbs.)
Height __ (ft.) _____ (in) = _____ (in)

The easiest way to get your BMI is to plug the numbers into an online calculator. *Google "BMI Calculator" for a long list of calculators.* If you prefer to go old school, use the formula below.

BMI = Weight (lbs.) / [Height (in.)]^2 x 703 *Using standard units*

BMI = Weight (kg)/ Height^2 (m) *Using metric units*

Example:
Calculate BMI for a 5'8" person who weighs 209 lbs.

$$BMI = 209 / (68)^2 \times 703 = 31.8$$

Calculate and record your BMI and find the associated weight range using the chart.

BMI = _____

Weight Range	BMI Category
Underweight	<18.5
Normal Weight	18.5 – 24.9
Overweight	25.0 – 29.9
Grade I Obesity	30.0 – 34.9
Grade II Obesity	35.0 – 39.9
Grade III Obesity	>40

Don't let labels alarm you. Consider this information an indication of your level of risk for weight-related conditions and diseases. Use this baseline feedback as fuel for improvement.

Note: BMI is an estimation that does not differentiate between overfat and a highly muscular body type. A tall, highly conditioned athlete can have the same BMI as a short, under-conditioned person with a large amount of body fat. For this reason, BMI should be considered in conjunction with other body composition measurement.

A special note to my African-American sisters—I repeatedly hear black women say BMI is not valid for us because of our body structure. The assertion is typically supported with an example that by BMI standards, Serena Williams is overweight. First, at 5'9" and 155 pounds (her weight at 2015 Wimbledon) Serena's BMI is 22.9, which is in the normal range, not overweight. Second, Serena's body is clearly a work of athletic excellence. She spends hours in the gym and on the tennis court. She is far from normal. The BMI estimations of body fat and related health risk do not apply to her. *For those of us who spend hours and hours in a chair, in a car, or on a couch, we are much closer to normal, so the charts may apply.*

Specifics like gender and ethnicity should be taken into account. Molly Bray, an associate professor of pediatrics at Baylor College of Medicine, states that the BMI scale "was created years ago and is based on Caucasian men and women. It doesn't take into account differences in body composition between genders, race/ethnicity groups, and across the life span."[10] Dr. Bray asserts that African-American women are not considered obese until a they have a BMI of 32 instead of 30.

In the absence of abundant details about BMI research on the African-American community, it is wise to consider the abundant information about African-Americans and health. For example, the Centers for Disease Control's *Health Disparities & Inequalities Report - United States, 2013* reports:

- African-American women had the largest prevalence of obesity as compared with white and Mexican American women and men (2007-2010).

- African-Americans had the highest death rates from heart disease and stroke compared with other racial and ethnic populations.

- The prevalence of diabetes among African-American adults was nearly twice as large as the prevalence among white adults (2010).

- The percentages of African-American adults who had control of high blood pressure were lower than among white adults (2007-2010).

- The decrease in number of years of expected life free of activity limitations caused by chronic conditions was less for African-American adults than white adults. (1999-2008).[11]

These and other life- and health-limiting conditions that disproportionately affect African-American men and women have a relationship to weight. Add to this the fact that many African-American women don't see their excess weight. "According to researchers in the study Body Size Perception among African-American Women, 56% of overweight women (BMI 25 or greater) and 40% of obese women (BMI 30 or greater) did not classify their body size as overweight, obese, or too fat."[12] Refusing to see the problem is a refusal to address the problem.

Stewardship calls for better. Don't let cultural norms or personal comfortability block potentially lifesaving feedback. Appropriately consider your BMI along with other health and body composition measures.

Waist Circumference

Waist circumference is often considered in conjunction with BMI. While BMI estimates the amount of fat, waist circumference is a non-intrusive indicator of excess belly fat that has been linked to increased risk of type 2 diabetes and heart disease. This measure is most useful for individuals with a BMI < 35.

To measure your waist circumference, stand up straight and encircle your body with a tape measure just above your hip bone at the level of your navel (not the middle or the smallest part of your waist). Breathe out, keep the tape straight, and pull it tight enough so it does not slip but not so tight as to cause an indentation in your flesh.

Health Risk	Waist Circumference Women	Waist Circumference Men
Low Risk	<35 inches	<40 inches
Increased Risk	35 inches or more	40 inches or more

Measure and record your waist circumference and find the associated health risk range using the chart.

My waist circumference = _____

Waist-to-Hip Ratio

Waist-to-hip ratio (WHR) is a similar helpful indicator of fat and related health risk.

To calculate your WHR:

Measure your waist. Stand up straight and encircle your abdomen with a tape measure at the smallest area of your waist (or just below the last rib). Breathe out, keep the tape level, and pull it tight enough so it does not slip but not so tight as to cause an indentation in your flesh. Record it below.

Waist = _____

Measure your hips. Stand up straight and encircle your body with a tape measure at the largest area around your hips and buttocks. Keep the tape level and pull tight enough so it does not slip but not so tight as to cause an indentation in your flesh. Record it below.

Hips = _____

Waist-to-Hip Ratio = waist / hips
Example: 27 in. / 38 in. = .71

Measure and record your waist circumference and find the associated WHR norm on the following chart.

Gender	Excellent	Good	Average	At Risk
Women	<0.75	0.75-0.79	0.80-0.86	>0.86
Men	<0.85	0.85-0.89	0.90-0.95	>0.95

My WHR = _____

Note: Need to whittle your waist? No number of sit-ups, crunches, or planks will do it alone. Spot reducing is a myth. Those exercises are good, and done consistently, they will tone and strengthen the abdominal and core muscles ... beneath the fat. Loss of fat requires a calorie deficit (explained in Chapter 3).

Other Methods of Body Composition Measurements

Skinfold measurements are an inexpensive and non-intrusive way to determine the percentage of body fat. This method is based on the assumption that roughly half of a person's body fat is under the skin. A personal trainer, health coach, or other health or fitness professional uses calipers to measure skinfolds at specific places on the body. The measurements are used in equations that produce an estimate of total body fat. When done correctly, this method has been found to be relatively accurate.[13]

Bioelectrical impedance is based on the principle that lean tissue conducts electricity easier than fatty tissue. A device passes a small electrical current through the body. The unit measures the resistance to the current and calculates body density and percentage of body fat. This method has been shown to be as accurate as skinfold measurements, provided the person measured stays still during the measurement and is well hydrated. This method is incorporated into many electronic body scales that provide body fat information.[14]

Hydrostatic weighing is a highly accurate and some say a highly inconvenient method of body composition measurement. It involves

41

submersion in a tank of water. Body density is calculated by relating normal body weight with underwater body weight.[15]

Dual energy x-ray absorptiometry (DEXA) measurement is a highly accurate method using a whole body scanner. Low-dose x-rays measure soft tissue and bone mass at the same time. Some call DEXA the benchmark of body composition measurement because it not only tells you how much body fat you have, but where the body fat is located.[16]

Pulling It Together

Weight with selected other measures of body composition gives an indication of current status and direction of needed change for improved health and wholeness. If you don't know where you are, how can you map the path to your goals? Once on that path, feedback is needed to keep moving in the right direction.

Plans fail for lack of counsel (Proverbs 15:22a). When it comes to something as important to physical stewardship as determining your healthy weight, the path to attain it, and how to live it—engage appropriate advisors. Time is up for Googling and guessing about your body. Take advantage of the help and resources God has provided to care for your earthly temple.

I regularly monitor my weight (almost daily), and a few times a year I record body measurements, lean body mass, and body fat using tools I have as a health coach. In addition to my annual physical, I get an InBody® full-body composition analysis and consult with my physician, Dr. Rani Whitfield. I selected Dr. Whitfield because of his Family Medicine specialty, Certificate of Added Qualification (CAQ) in Sports Medicine, and his focus on health awareness and disease prevention. Dr. Whitfield informs and calls his patients to drive their health with the appropriate emphasis on sound nutrition and focused consistent exercise.

Pull together a team to help you find your healthy weight and support your weight loss and maintenance efforts. With the Holy Spirit as your guide, engage your healthcare provider, registered dietitian, exercise professional, and health coach. Sideline Dr. Google (without due diligence, he can lead you wrong) and anyone who is comfortable with you staying where you are.

Notes:

At the time of this writing, under the Affordable Care Act, diet counseling for adults at higher risk for chronic disease is a preventative service covered at 100% without a copayment, co-insurance or deductible requirements.[17] Check with your insurance provider for details on how you can see a registered dietitian for personalized nutrition information to support your weight loss efforts.

Health coaching is a relatively new profession created to address the rise of overweight and obesity. Health coaches work with people struggling with obstacles that have kept them from eating better, moving more, and making their health a priority. These professionals have the behavior change, physical activity, and nutrition coaching skills to empower people to long-term healthy change.[18]

Examine Thyself

At the opening of this chapter, the question was posed, "What pulls on you as a result of the size and condition of your body?" In addition to physical pounds, what other weight will you release?

Detail your initial thoughts regarding your healthy weight.

Consider your weight history. What weight set points have you experienced? Complete the chart below. (Note highs as well as lows.)

Weight Set Point	Period	Conditions or behaviors	Effect
Label with weight, clothing size, age, or other description.	When were you at this weight? How long did you maintain?	What behaviors or conditions contributed to this weight set point?	How did you feel physically at this set point?

Record your weight progress. Use this chart to record progress for the next 12 months.

Date	Weight	BMI	Waist Circ. or WHR	Other Measure	Notes

Date	Weight	BMI	Waist Circ. or WHR	Other Measure	Notes

Praction (Prayer - Action)

Journal your thoughts, prayer, and plan of action from this section.

CHAPTER 3

The Science of Weight Loss

I praise you because I am fearfully and wonderfully made;
your works are wonderful, I know that full well.
Psalm 134:14

My people are destroyed from lack of knowledge.
Hosea 4:6a

IN ESSENCE, WEIGHT MANAGEMENT boils down to energy management.

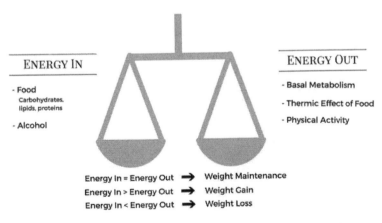

We take in energy from food and drink in the form of carbohydrates, lipids (fats), and proteins.

We expend energy in three main ways. Our basal metabolism (BEE) is the amount of energy our body needs to rest, maintain body temperature, and survive. Many factors impact BEE. For example, BEE decreases with age, when a person has consistently reduced caloric intake or when a person has too little thyroid hormone (hypothyroidism). BEE increases with stimulant use, during pregnancy, or with increased lean body mass (men tend to have more muscle and thus have higher metabolisms than most women).

The thermic effect of food (TEF) is the energy required to digest and absorb nutrients from food and drink. Some foods are harder to digest and absorb, and thus, the TEF burn is higher. Meals that include lean protein and high-fiber carbohydrate foods will have a higher TEF than meals comprising primarily refined carbohydrates and fats.

Physical activity also requires energy, including energy requirements for basic movement as well as intentional exercise.

You may find the breakdown of energy expenditure interesting. BEE is typically 60 to 75 percent of a person's total energy use. TEF makes up approximately 10 percent, and physical activity uses 15 to 30 percent of daily energy expenditures typically. BEE and TEF are not as easily controlled as physical activity.

Energy Out

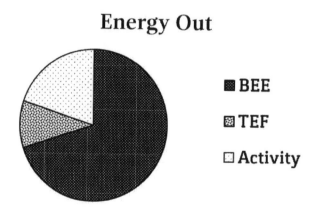

- BEE
- TEF
- Activity

When energy consumed matches the energy used, body weight is maintained. When a person takes in more energy than she burns, the excess energy is stored, and there is weight gain. Then there is the sweet spot for weight loss—when more energy is expended than consumed, the body turns to stored energy and weight is lost.

This simple balance equation becomes complex when we consider other contributing factors. Weight loss is also affected by:

- **Genetics.** Science confirms that genes play a role in weight management. For example, on the weight loss side, the uncoupling protein-2 gene (UCP2) activates a protein that burns excess calories as heat. High activity of this gene may block fat storage. On the weight gain side, research supports that some people are genetically predisposed to store extra calories as fat. However, other factors (i.e., overconsumption of food, lack of physical exercise, etc.) must also be present for the overweight/obese condition to occur.

- **Environment.** The setup and conditions of where a person lives, works, shops, and gets medical care affect weight management. The environment can support or hinder healthy behaviors.

- **Social and economic factors.** Cultural norms, marketing influences, and methods of entertainment impact weight management. Obesity rates are higher in lower socio-economic populations. Reduced access to healthy foods, abundant access to low-cost, calorie-dense processed foods, and limited access to safe areas to exercise make losing weight difficult.

- **Drugs.** Some medications like steroids or antidepressants can cause weight gain. Stimulants can cause weight loss.

- **Medical conditions** can also impact weight. Polycystic ovarian syndrome, hypothyroidism, and Cushing's syndrome can cause weight gain.

Some factors that control weight management are beyond our control. Don't worry about those. We can't control what we can't control. With God's help, we can control what we can control. Do that and live at your healthy weight.

> *Don't worry about anything; instead, pray about everything. Tell God what you need, and thank him for all he has done.* Philippians 4:6 NLT

Let's qualify and quantify concepts with a few definitions and calculations.

Calories

Nutritional energy is measured in calories. A calorie is the amount of energy required to raise one gram of water by one degree Celsius. Calories come in the form of carbohydrates, fats, and protein.

Carbohydrates

Carbohydrates, the body's preferred energy source, contain four calories per gram. Carbohydrates are the sugars (monosaccharide, disaccharide, oligosaccharide, or polysaccharide), starches, and fiber found primarily in plants and milk products. (Fiber has zero calories). Carbohydrates are essential for brain function and provide energy to muscle tissue and the nervous system.

Carbohydrates are classified as simple and complex. Complex carbohydrates are typically fruits, vegetables, and grains that are close to their natural state. They are rich in fiber, meaning they slow digestion and keep blood sugar more stable. Examples include green vegetables, beans and legumes, whole-grain foods (i.e., whole-grain pasta or bread) and starchy vegetables (i.e., squash, corn, pumpkin, and potatoes). While complex carbs generally come from plants (vegetation), simple carbs are often made in plants (manufacturing). Simple carbohydrates are easily digested energy sources like table sugar, candy, soft drinks, etc. Natural sources of simple carbohydrates include honey, molasses, and fruit juices.

The best carbohydrate sources for weight loss are those that are less processed. During processing, the food is broken down, fiber and other essential nutrients are often removed, and salt, sugar, and fat are added.

Not-So-Great Carb Choice	Better Carb Choice	Super-Duper Carb Choice
Candy	Dried Fruit	Fresh Fruit
Sugary Cereal	Whole-Grain or Bran Cereal or Instant Oatmeal	Oatmeal Made from Old Fashioned or Steel Cut Oats
White Rice	Brown Rice	Quinoa
Smushy White Bread (the kind that holds your finger indentions)	Whole-Wheat Bread	Multi-Grain Bread
Buttery Cracker	Whole-Grain Cracker	Vegetable Crudité
Soft Drink	Fruit Juice	Sparkling Water with a Splash of Fruit Juice

Your turn. List three to five simple or processed carbs you regularly eat or drink. Then complete the table with complex or less processed options.

Not-So-Great Carb Choice	Better Carb Choice	Super-Duper Carb Choice
_____	_____	_____
_____	_____	_____
_____	_____	_____
_____	_____	_____
_____	_____	_____

Protein

Protein, the building blocks of the body, also contain four calories per gram. Built from a combination of 20 amino acids, protein forms muscle, blood, skin, hair, the nervous system, and the brain.

When you say protein, most people think of foods that had mothers (pork, poultry, beef, fish, etc.). Other protein sources include eggs, milk products, beans, nuts, tofu, soybean products (soymilk, tempeh), and seitan (protein derived from wheat).

Proteins are classified as complete and incomplete. Recall that proteins are made of 20 amino acids. Our bodies can produce 11 of the 20. The other nine the body can't produce, and it is essential that they come from food. They are called essential acids. Complete proteins contain all nine essential acids. Incomplete proteins do not. Animal proteins are complete proteins. Soy products, quinoa, chia, amaranth, and hemp are also complete proteins. Most other plant proteins are incomplete. Individuals following a plant-based diet are encouraged to combine foods to get all amino acids.

Another classification more useful to weight loss and maintenance is lean protein. Unfortunately, the most commonly eaten protein sources also contain significant amounts of fat and cholesterol that are not beneficial for health or weight loss. Lean proteins contain sensible amounts of fat and cholesterol. The USDA defines lean protein as having up to 10 grams of total fat, 4.5 grams or less of saturated fat and less than 95 milligrams of cholesterol in a 3.5-ounce portion.

Popular lean protein selections include beans and legumes; skinless chicken or turkey; many seafood options, including tuna, tilapia and salmon; eggs; and low-fat dairy products. Twenty cuts of beef meet the lean protein guideline, including brisket flat half, flank steak, sirloin center cut roast, top sirloin steak, round roasts, round steak, shoulder roasts, tenderloin steak, and T-bone steak. For ground beef, 90 percent lean or greater is a lean protein. Lean pork selections include tenderloin, sirloin roast, and loin chops.

Keep lean proteins lean with your preparation. A lean cut of meat or seafood that is fried or pan fried and smothered in gravy is no longer lean. For healthy weight loss, broil, boil, grill, roast, poach, or steam.

Your turn. List three to five of your favorite protein foods and preparations (for example, grilled T-bone, smothered pork chop). If the item is not lean, brainstorm ways you can slim it down (to slim you down).

Favorite Protein Entrée	Is It Lean?	Slimmed Selection or Preparation
	❏ Yes! ❏ Nope.	
	❏ Yes! ❏ Nope.	
	❏ Yes! ❏ Nope.	
	❏ Yes! ❏ Nope.	
	❏ Yes! ❏ Nope.	

Dietary Fat

Fat contains nine calories per gram. Fat gets an awful rap, but we need fat in our body and diet. Fat provides energy, energy storage, and insulation that protects our organs. Fat supports the absorption of fat-soluble vitamins A, D, E, and K, and it enables nerve transmission and hormone production. On the pleasure side, fat also adds richness to meals. It has a mouth feel that many enjoy, and it helps satiety.

Fat does not make you fat. For years, the low-fat food movement drove this belief into consumers' heads. On the market popped thousands of fat-free products that were loaded with excess sugar and salt (to make up for the missing fat). As a result, many fat-free products contain as many calories as their full-fat counterparts. People who thought, "It's fat-free, so it's less fattening," ate up and often gained weight. Personally, I think the taste and texture of many manipulated fat-free items are substandard. I'll take a smaller amount of real cheese over fat-free cheese food any day. Ditto regarding mayonnaise and salad dressings.

That said, the amount of fat consumed should not be excessive. Fat has a high-calorie density, with 225 percent the calories of the same amount of protein or carbohydrate. For weight loss and maintenance, try to keep the amount of fat in your eating reasonable.

For health, consideration also should be made regarding the type of fat: monounsaturated, polyunsaturated, saturated, or trans fat. Some have health benefits. Others are harmful to health and should be avoided.

Type of Fat	Source	Qualities	Recommended Intake
Monounsaturated Fat	Plant-based including olives, nuts, and avocados	Typically liquid at room temperature	15-20% of total daily fat intake
Polyunsaturated Fat	Plant-based including safflower, sunflower, corn, soybean, cottonseed, and nuts	Typically liquid at room temperature	5-10% of total daily fat intake
Saturated Fat	Animal-based fat and tropical plants	Typically waxy or solid at room temperature	<10% of total daily fat intake
Trans Fat	Manufactured by hydrogenating liquid fat into a solid	Used by manufacturers to change the feel of the product and increase shelf life	0% Trans fats are bad.

Trans fats raise levels of "bad" cholesterol (LDL) and reduce levels of "good" cholesterol (HDL). They have been deemed unsafe for human consumption and this year, the FDA passed regulation giving manufacturers three years to remove all partially hydrogenated oils from foods. Check the labels of purchased foods. Trans fats may still be in margarine, shortening, convenience foods (including chips and french fries), and baked goods.

Review the list on the following page of ways to reduce fat intake.

Check tips you currently use or are willing to try.

Use the space below to record new ideas that come to mind.

	10 Easy Steps to Reduce Dietary Fat Intake
❏	Use ½ the amount of fat specified in non-baking recipes.
❏	Substitute pureed fruit for a portion of oil, shortening, or butter in baking recipes. *Applesauce, ripe banana, and pureed fruit work very well.*
❏	Choose hummus, flavored mustard, guacamole, or Greek yogurt as a spread instead of mayonnaise. *These options add moisture and creaminess, plus a punch of flavor.*
❏	Put away the butter dish. *Often we slap on a pat of butter from habit. For example, try oatmeal or grits without extra butter.*
❏	Grill or roast meat and vegetables instead of deep frying. *You will taste the actual food instead of fried batter crust.*
❏	Serve salad dressing on the side. *Dip your fork into the dressing, and then spear salad greens.*
❏	Degrease gravies and soups before eating. *Use a skimmer cup or refrigerate. The fat will coagulate on top. Peel it off and discard.*
❏	Do not save bacon drippings or other expelled animal fat for "seasoning." *Actual seasonings (herbs, spices, etc.) work beautifully. Really, they do. Give them a chance.*
❏	Use a 3:1 egg white-to-egg ratio in your omelets, scrambled eggs, and frittatas. *Your eggs will have volume, flavor, and a lot of protein without a lot of fat or cholesterol.*
❏	Use avocado instead of butter on toast or on top of a baked potato.

Nutrition labels, online nutrition databases, or apps make it easy to access information on how much energy you take in your body.

We have looked into calories in; now let's add some detail to calories out.

Calculate your Energy Needs[19]

Have you ever wondered how many calories you burn every day? This information is helpful for energy balance. While I do not recommend counting calories for everything you eat, drink, and what you burn every day for the rest of your life (*does that sound livable to you?*), background knowledge of these numbers is a great baseline to keep eating and activity in check.

First, for most people, this number is an approximation. To accurately calculate calorie burn requires fasting state analysis of your oxygen intake and carbon dioxide output. This requires a metabolic cart that runs $20,000 to $50,000. We'll use a few tables and equations instead.

The simplest method uses your gender, weight, and a multiplier to estimate total daily caloric requirements. This is a ballpark of how many calories a person burns in a day.

Gender	Light Activity	Moderate Activity	Heavy Activity
Women	16	17	30
Men	17	19	23

Light activity - Walking (0 incline, 2.5-3.0 mph), housecleaning, child care, golf
Moderate activity - Walking (3.5-4.0 mph), cycling, skiing, tennis, dancing
Heavy activity - Walking uphill, basketball, climbing, football, soccer

Source: Nutritional Programming by Debra Wein, M.S., R.D., L.D.N, C.S.S.D, NSCA-CPT

First, determine what your overall daily activity level looks like (light, medium, or heavy). *Notice, this is your overall level. A person who has a desk job and is basically sedentary most of the day but does a killer hour workout three to four days per week would be in the light category most of the time. One hour of high activity a day does not counteract the other 23 low-activity hours. If not sure, pick two activity levels and calculate a range.*

Next, take your current weight in pounds and multiply it by the number in the cell at the intersection for your gender and activity. Burn approximately this many calories per day and weight will be maintained. Burn more and/or eat less, and weight loss should occur. Eat more and/or burn less, and weight gain main be on the way.

Example: A 220-pound woman with a light activity level requires approximately 3,520 calories to maintain her weight (220 x 16 = 3,520).

Fitness professionals often choose from a set of equations to estimate basal metabolic rate. Earlier in this chapter, basal metabolism (BEE, also called BMR) was introduced as the amount of energy your body uses to function and keep you alive (approximately 60 to 75 percent of your daily caloric expenditure). These calculations tell approximately how much you burn at rest. Excluding activity calories makes the calorie balance easier for people who regularly exercise (as we all should!).

Note: Some of the calculations are a bit involved. For ease, Google the name of the equations and use one of the free online calculators.

Harris-Benedict Equation

This method tends to underestimate BMR in women and overestimate BMR in men. First, complete the base BMR calculation.

Men:
BMR = 66 + (6.2 x weight in lbs.) + (12.7 x height in inches) – (6.76 x age in years)

Women:
BMR = 655.1 + (4.35 x weight in lbs.) + (4.7 x height in inches) - (4.7 x age in years)

Next, factor in overall activity by multiplying the BMR by an activity factor: 1.2 = bed rest, 1.3 = sedentary, 1.4 = active, 1.5 = very active.

Mifflin-St. Jeor Equation

This method tends to yield a better approximation for obese people vs. non-obese people. Convert height and weight to metric units for this equation. First, complete the base BMR calculation.

Men:
BMR = (9.99 x weight in kg.) + (6.25 x height in cm) - (4.92 x age in years) + 5

Women:
BMR = (9.99 x weight in kg.) + (6.25 x height in cm) - (4.92 x age in years) - 161

Next, factor in overall activity by multiplying the BMR by an activity factor: 1.2 = sedentary (very little exercise), 1.375 = light exercise (light workout 1-3 days per week), 1.550 = moderately active (moderate exercise 3-5 days per week), 1.725 = very active (hard exercise 6-7 days per week), 1.900 = extra active (very hard exercise and a physically demanding job).

Schofield Equation

This simpler equation yields a slight underestimate for women and overestimate for men. Convert height and weight to metric units for his equation.

Age	Men	Women
18-30	BMR = (15 x weight in kg) + 690	BMR = (14.8 x weight in kg) + 485
30-60	BMR = (11.4 x weight in kg) + 870	BMR = (8.1 x weight in kg) + 842
>60	BMR = (11.7 x weight in kg) + 585	BMR = (9 x weight in kg) + 656

Cunningham Equation

This equation is often used by fitness professionals to estimate BMR for athletes. Fat-free mass (FFM) is used for this estimation.
BMR = (21.6 x FFM in kg) +370

Select a method and record your total daily calorie expenditure or BMR.

My total calorie expenditure _____

My BMR _____

Overweight or Overfat

Body weight is made of fat and fat-free mass (FFM), also called lean body mass (LBM). Fat-free mass includes body water (intracellular and extracellular—inside and outside of cells), muscle, and organ tissue and bone. The goal of healthy weight loss is to lose primarily fat mass. Extreme methods including high-calorie restriction or over-exercise can pull FFM from our body.

Let's get to know our target better.

Five Fat Facts

Fat, also called adipose tissue, is an energy store equivalent to 3,500 calories per pound.

Adipose tissue is categorized by color.

White fat stores energy and produces hormones. White fat is the most common type of fat in the body.

Brown fat can actually burn calories when stimulated. More common in children than adults, and thin people than overweight or obese people, brown fat helps keep us warm.

Fat is also categorized by location.

Visceral fat is deep fat that surrounds our organs. This fat is not healthy. It drives insulin resistance and is linked to heart disease, stroke, and dementia. A large waist circumference is an indicator of significant amounts of visceral fat.

Subcutaneous fat is the fat just under the skin. While unsightly, the health impacts are not as harmful as visceral fat (unless the subcutaneous fat is on the belly).

Belly fat is a combination of visceral and subcutaneous fat. It carries similar health risks to visceral fat.

Hip and thigh fat are typically subcutaneous fat. Women who are pear shaped (more fat in the hip and thigh area) are less likely to develop metabolic disease than women with an apple shape (more fat in the belly area).

Lost fat doesn't really go away. Fat cells just shrink.

Think of fat cells like balloons. They begin to form before birth, and when we enter puberty, sex hormones spur the creation of fat cells in different areas of the body based upon gender. Men tend to carry more in the abdomen and chest, women more in the breasts, hips, waist, and butt. Once set, the number of fat cells in our bodies stays roughly the same throughout adulthood (with slight increases during pregnancy).

As we gain weight, the cells (balloons) fill and puff up with fat. When we lose weight, the fat cells deflate. Researchers suggest this is a contributing factor to why many weight losers can regain weight easily. The "balloons" are there waiting to be refilled.

Another implication being explored is the importance of prevention of childhood obesity. Children that enter adulthood with a high density of fat cells in their body may face stronger challenges maintaining a healthy weight.

Small Changes Lead to Big Results

One hundred calories isn't much, right? Five peppermints, two slices of bacon, a small glass of sweet tea, half a Krispy Kreme donut—each of these is about 100 calories.

A habit of only 100 extra calories per day could cause a 10-pound weight gain in a year. Let's do the math.

1 pound of body fat = 3,500 calories
100 extra calories per day = 700 extra calories per week
700 calories/week x 52 weeks = 36,200 extra calories in a year

Since these calories are extra, they are stored as fat.
36,200 calories / 3,500 calories/pound = 10.4 pounds

Pick up two sacks of potatoes and throw them across your shoulders. A simple, mindless habit of a few peppermints popped in your mouth every day can put this weight on your body.

Now, repeat this small habit for five years and be prepared to carry 50 extra pounds.

A tad depressing? But wait! There's more.

A deficit of only 100 calories per day could cause a semi-mindless 10-pound weight loss in a year or 50 pounds from your frame in five years. This is shouting news!

A 100-calorie daily deficit is easily accomplished. Make a simple food or beverage swap (for example, drink water or unsweet tea instead of sweet tea), or burn an extra 100 calories per day with activity. In general, a 20-minute walk at 3.0 mph, 15 minutes of vigorous dancing, or a half hour of playing with children can burn 100 calories.

This is so good and powerful. Let's bring this to life in your life.

Set a timer for two minutes. Pray for guidance and an open mind.

In the first table, brainstorm foods, beverages, or additions to foods or beverages you consume almost every day. Don't think big, think about the small things. The two teaspoons of sugar added to your daily cup of joe. The bowl of candy at the office you dip into every day. The piece of cheese on your sandwich or burger. Think regulars in your diet.

Ready? Start the timer and go.

Small and Regular Eats and Drinks

Reset the timer for three minutes. Pray for guidance and an open mind. In the next table, list swaps or changes to items in the first table—and list only ones that you are willing to make. Also, list small, fun ways to add bits of activity to your day. Don't worry about the calorie counts or equivalents right now. You are brainstorming possibilities.

Ready? Start the timer and go.

```
┌─────────────────────────────────────────────┐
│ ┌───────────────────────────────────────┐   │
│ │ Small Swaps to Regular Eats and Drinks │   │
│ │         and Activity Adds              │   │
│ └───────────────────────────────────────┘   │
│                                               │
│                                               │
│                                               │
│                                               │
│                                               │
│                                               │
│                                               │
│                                               │
│                                               │
│                                               │
│                                               │
│                                               │
│                                               │
│                                               │
└─────────────────────────────────────────────┘
```

Keep these options in mind. Add to the list—and make the swaps. It doesn't have to be the same swap every day. The consistent goal is to achieve a simple 100-calorie deficit per day. The way you get that deficit is variable.

The main takeaway is to become conscious of what you eat and drink and make daily choices that benefit your body and stewardship goals.

Share the small changes you are making. I'd enjoy seeing what you are doing, and the sharing may give someone else inspiration or helpful ideas. Tweet your change to @nettyejohnson with the hashtag #TempleCare.

Make It Last

The vast majority of people who lose weight gain it back. Estimates vary, but I've seen reports indicating as high as 80 to 95 percent of losers regain all the lost weight back.

Join the faithful few that don't regain.

First let's look at what doesn't work. Following are five elements research indicates lead to yo-yo weight. Be aware and make appropriate adjustments so these weight loss saboteurs do not sabotage your success.

- **Working one side of the energy balance.** Focusing on diet only without regular exercise or regularly exercising without attention to eating. In general, 70 to 75 percent of weight loss is due to nutrition. (It is really hard to outrun, out-bike or out-Zumba an out-of-balance diet). Nonetheless, successful weight maintenance after a loss requires increased activity as well.

- **Loss of fat-free mass (FFM).** Not all weight loss is body fat. Water and muscle are also lost. If weight loss is too rapid or not balanced with exercises that build muscle, muscle loss can occur. Less muscle lowers the BMR, which makes weight gain easier. Sensible nutrition and balanced exercise will preserve FFM.

- **Adaptive thermogenesis** is the body's automatic reduction in energy expenditure. This frequently happens when we lose weight. The body wants to stabilize and stop weight reduction, so the energy expenditure slows. The amount of calories that used to maintain weight may begin to cause weight gain. To combat this, as the body adjusts, adjust behaviors. Increase activity or adjust food intake to maintain the desired weight.

- **Approaching weight loss with the wrong mindset.** Diet mentality is a setup for regain. (See Chapter 1.)

- **Living in a state of stress.** Stress eating can bring on pounds. Internally, stress triggers adrenal responses. When stressed, the body releases the hormone cortisol. Excess cortisol pulls from muscle mass and causes the storage of fat.

A Big Group of Losers

From the National Weight Control Registry website (www.nwcr.ws)

The National Weight Control Registry (NWCR) is the largest perspective investigation of long-term weight loss maintenance. Given the prevailing belief that few individuals succeed at long-term weight loss, the NWCR was developed to identify and investigate the characteristics of individuals who have succeeded at long-term weight loss. The NWCR is tracking over 10,000 individuals who have lost significant amounts of weight and kept it off for long periods of time. Detailed questionnaires and annual follow-up surveys are used to examine the behavioral and psychological characteristics of weight maintainers, as well as the strategies they use to maintain their weight losses.

I am a member of the NWCR study. The group is very diverse. Many different methods were used to lose weight, but researchers find some commonalities in how successful losers keep the weight off.

Check out five NCWR-substantiated healthy habits and incorporate elements that fit in your lifestyle now.

1. Modify food intake in some way. Most of the successful maintainers made some permanent changes to the way they eat.

2. Increase physical activity. Ninety percent of NWCR participants exercise an average of 420 minutes per week (about 1 hour per day). Note that the most common exercise reported among the successful weight losers and maintainers is walking.

3. Eat breakfast. Seventy-eight percent report eating breakfast every day. Ninety percent report eating breakfast at least five days per week.

4. Weigh at least once per week. Regular feedback enables adjustments to offset weight fluctuations.

5. Watch less than 10 hours of TV per week. Studies indicate the more TV people watch, the more likely they are to gain weight.

Praction (Prayer - Action)

Journal your thoughts, prayer, and plan of action from this section.

CHAPTER 4

Weight Loss Begins in the Mind
Get Rid of Those ANTs!

For as he thinketh ... so is he.
Proverbs 23:7 (KJV)

"Get the mind right. The butt (and gut) will follow."
Nettye Johnson

I DO NOT LIKE insects—especially not in my space. When a mosquito gets in the house, I think of West Nile and everyone has to get a towel, shoe, or something and go after it until it is no more. If I see a spider, someone has to get the long hose attachment on the vacuum to get rid of it (I don't want anyone to get close and risk it jumping on them when they try to kill it). And I can't even look at a water bug. They give me the willies and send me running.

As much as I don't like insects, I seldom react when I see an ant in my home. Perhaps it is because they are so small, or the fact that I see them out and about regularly. I just don't take pause. Despite their harmless size and appearance, these little creatures can be dangerous.

- Consider their strength—an ant can lift 20 times its size.
- Consider their social nature—when one ant is seen, if it finds a habitable environment, its friends will quickly come in large numbers.
- Consider their ability to multiply—a single queen ant can have millions of babies.

- Consider their laser focus—each ant is focused on a single job and it will work unto death to get it accomplished.

Ants can spoil food and destroy structures. They should not be taken lightly.

The same can be said for another kind of ANT—the **Automatic Negative Thought**. These are the defeating self-pronouncements that run across our mind, and depending on the company, may come out of our mouth.

- "I'm fat!"
- "I can't lose this weight."
- "The struggle is real. Losing weight is too hard!"
- "Diabetes runs in my family. There's nothing I can do about it."
- "I've always been big. No use trying. I'm fine with my weight."
- "I can't stop _____" (You fill in the blank.)
- "I could never _____" (Again, you fill in the blank.)
- _____
- _____
- _____

How often do negative thoughts come into our space (minds) and we overlook—or even worse—tacitly believe them? Perhaps because we assume that little thoughts can't affect much.

The Bible warns of the power of thoughts. Proverbs 23:7 tells us as a man thinketh, so is he.

Negative thoughts, like the insect ant, do damage. They multiply, and piece by piece, they break down and carry off the fruit God has given you.

As this relates to health and weight loss, a positive progressive mind is critical. Daniel Amen, M.D., the author of *Change Your Brain, Change Your Body,* calls the brain the control center of your body. He states, "One of the most effective solutions for improving every aspect of your body is learning to use new thinking skills to help your weight, health, beauty and fitness goals."[20] For healthy cognitive skills and thoughts to take root, the persistent and destructive thoughts have to go. They can have no place in your mind.

So how do we get rid of the ANTs?

Many psychology experts suggest immediately flipping the script. Talk right back to yourself, changing that negative thought to a positive. Sometimes this is easier said than done, particularly if the damage done is not acknowledged or addressed.

Philippians 4:6-7 provides another process to get rid of those ANTs.

> Do not be anxious about anything, but in every situation, by prayer and petition, with thanksgiving, present your requests to God. [7]And the peace of God, which transcends all understanding, will guard your hearts and your minds in Christ Jesus."
> Philippians 4:6-7

In times of an unsettled mind, these scriptures direct us to God with prayers of thanksgiving.

When a negative thought enters speaking lies about who we are or what we cannot do, don't begin by talking back to yourself. First, talk to God.

God knows the end.

He sees the battles won, the strongholds broken, and His purposes fulfilled.

God is our Strength. As children of the Most High, we don't have to fight any battle alone—not even a battle with our own mind!

Beloved, the struggle is real, but not necessary. We worry, beat ourselves up, and struggle with weight because we choose to struggle. God desires we be in good health (3 John 2). Struggle around the blessing He has for us is a distraction. It is a fruitless, senseless use of mental and emotional energy.

The struggle is real, but not necessary.

Place that which troubles our mind in His hands, thanking Him for what He has done and will do (Philippians 4:6). Instead of lamenting about where we are, thank God for sustaining us. Consider a few examples:

Frustrated over thick thighs? Thank God those thick thighs hold you up and move you where you need to go. Then move them more with some exercise.

Feeling defeated by the talking to from your doctor about your blood pressure and labs? Thank God for that heart and each of the 115,200 times it beats every day. Then let faith and thankfulness move you to sit less, move more, make heart-healthy food choices, and be consistently compliant with your medications and follow-ups.

Today, your body and health may not be where they could or should be, but you are here. God granted another day, another chance, another opportunity to do better so you can feel and be better. Instead of focusing on what you don't have, thank Him in advance for what He will bring.

When we replace worry or negative thoughts with thankful prayer and supplication, we surrender, connect, and agree with God. In response, look at what our awesome God promises. His Word says He will give us peace (Philippians 4:7). A peace that passes all understanding. A peace that will guard and keep our hearts and minds.

Now, with the negative thoughts gone and the balm of peace applied, we are directed (and able) to fill our minds with uplifting thoughts.

Finally, brothers and sisters, whatever is true, whatever is noble, whatever is right, whatever is pure, whatever is lovely, whatever is admirable—if anything is excellent or praiseworthy—think about such things. Philippians 4:8 NIV

Have ANTs found their way into your space? Take action:

1. Pray for awareness and begin to take note of defeating thoughts that come across your mind.
2. When the thought occurs, replace the thought with anticipatory prayers of thanksgiving until you experience God's peace.

3. Fill your mind with God's truth and uplifting thoughts.

4. Repeat, repeat, repeat.

Examine Thyself

Prayerfully reflect on self-defeating thoughts about your weight, eating, health, or other aspects of physical stewardship. List as many as come to mind in the chart below. In the next column, list uplifting responses (scripture, quotes, or other statements of truth).

Periodically revisit this list, noting when the negative thoughts listed no longer cross your mind. *That is praise break time!*

Defeating Thought	Uplifting Truth

Praction (Prayer - Action)

Journal your thoughts, prayer, and plan of action from this chapter.

NOURISH
YOUR BODY

CHAPTER 5

Foundations for Healthy Weight Maintenance

Therefore everyone who hears these words of mine and puts them into practice is like a wise man who built his house on the rock. [25] The rain came down, the streams rose, and the winds blew and beat against that house; yet it did not fall, because it had its foundation on the rock. [26] But everyone who hears these words of mine and does not put them into practice is like a foolish man who built his house on sand. [27] The rain came down, the streams rose, and the winds blew and beat against that house, and it fell with a great crash.
Matthew 7:24-27

MANY PEOPLE BUILD THEIR eating behaviors on sand, on a foundation that is not stable—eating patterns that shift, float along with currents of cravings, blown about by gusts of new information, and easily moved by tides of popular diet programs and fads.

There is so much information and it changes so often that knowing what to eat for health and weight management can be confusing.

The egg has gone from "incredible edible" good for you ("eat eggs!") to not good for you ("balls of cholesterol bad for your heart") to partly good, partly bad for you ("eat the whites, not the yolks") back to eat the whole egg ("Ahhh, eat 'em if you want–you'll be alright").

Margarine and butter have been duking it out for decades to be named the better spread for your bread. Then newbie olive oil and coconut oil spreads pop in the game. Folks just want something that tastes good and won't give them heart disease to moisten their toast!

The thing is, we live in the information age. Our brains are bombarded with data day in and day out. In 2010, Google ex-CEO Eric Schmidt estimated, "Every two days now we create as much information as we did from the dawn of civilization up until 2003."[21] Via the internet, 24-hour TV, radio news, and social media, we are uber-informed.

The human mind is amazing. When exposed, it absorbs and stores information even when we are not aware. This poses a challenge when significant portions of what we get is not true, beneficial, or applicable.

Relate this info overload to the important life issues of health, nutrition, and weight management. The determination and dissemination of food/health relationships, nutrition guidelines, and recommendations—really helpful information we'd hope would be black and white—is more often presented in 50 shades of gray. It is far too easy to be tossed to and fro by the waves of information.

Do not conform to the pattern of this world, but be transformed by the renewing of your mind. Then you will be able to test and approve what God's will is—his good, pleasing and perfect will. Romans 12:2

It benefits us to challenge and confirm things that enter our minds.

Progress to positive change is hindered when we go with the flow. It benefits us to challenge and confirm things that enter our minds.

I've discovered that principles used to study and rightly divide scripture help evaluate information, separate fact from fiction, and determine life application in many areas. Applying just a few of these methods to health information makes general truths evident and guides us to the specific fit for individual progress.

Step 1: Be like the Bereans

[10]As soon as it was night, the believers sent Paul and Silas away to Berea. On arriving there, they went to the Jewish synagogue. [11]Now the Berean Jews were of more noble character than those in Thessalonica, for they received the message with great eagerness and examined the Scriptures every day to see if what Paul said was true. [12]As a result, many of them believed, as did also a number of prominent Greek women and many Greek men. Acts 17:10-12

In his five missionary journeys, the Apostle Paul taught and ministered to people in over 50 towns. In some places, people challenged and rejected his teaching. In other towns, people were willing to hear but lacked zeal.

Then there were the Bereans. Scripture tells us the Berean Jews had an eagerness for the Word of God. They readily received the message—but note, they didn't just take what they heard Paul say and roll with it. The Word says they examined the scriptures every day, to make sure what they heard was true.

To get impact of their actions, picture the times. The canon of scripture we have today was not yet complete. During this time, people did not have Bibles in their homes. They didn't have commentaries, cross references, or topical dictionaries. They couldn't whip out their smartphone or tablet and quickly pull up the Holy written text for confirmation. As a matter of fact, few people in this time could read or write. Their access, resources, and helps for scriptural study were nothing like we have today. This did not squelch their eagerness. They put in the diligence to confirm, learn, and understand.

This desire and action was blessed. Verse 12 tells us as a result, many believed. Souls were saved. Their noble character is recorded forever in scripture.

The example shown in the three verses about the Bereans calls for a look at our zeal for life-changing knowledge.

With the indwelling of the Holy Spirit and all the helps and resources at our fingertips, how diligent are we in the study of God's

Word? What would an observer say about our character? Are souls being saved and lives being changed?

Now take it to the physical.

God's Word speaks to all areas of our lives, and if applied, the power of Berean behavior can manifest in our health and wellness.

- Have a thyroid issue that makes weight loss difficult? Berean behavior is eager for information on the condition.

- Your primary care physician, dietician, and endocrinologist share messages of weight loss and lifestyle changes that can manage or possibly reverse your diabetes? Berean behavior receives the information, checks it out, and gives it daily focus.

- A Facebook post says drinking baking soda with apple cider vinegar a couple times a day reduces blood pressure. Berean behavior doesn't rush to try it without research.

When presented with messages that directly impact the physical stewardship of your body, ask yourself:

- Am I open and eager to receive this information?

- Do I examine what is heard or read to confirm its validity or fit for my situation?

- Do I put in the focus and work so the good information progresses to belief and belief leads to change?

If information can help your health or weight loss efforts, don't refuse to move or move too soon. Be Berean about it.

Step 2: Consider the Context

In *How to Study the Bible*, Bible scholar John McArthur writes, "Once you read the Bible and know what it says, the next step is to find out what it means. Only when you've correctly interpreted a biblical passage can you apply it to your life and bring glory to God."[22] An important element of Biblical hermeneutics (principles and practice of biblical interpretation) is context. Meaning of scripture text becomes clearer when we consider:

- **pretext** – scripture before the selected verse.

- **post-text** – scripture after the selected text.

- **author** – background and character about the person God used to pen the scripture.

- **original audience** – who the scripture was originally written for.

- **purpose** – why it was written.

- **historical background and cultural environment** – the frame of reference for understanding.

- **harmony of scripture** – how this scripture agrees with other scripture and its fit in progressive relation of the Bible.

Scripture in isolation is open for misinterpretation. Context sets the scene and reveals the flow of thought of the message.

In isolation, *"By His stripes we are healed,"* from Isaiah 53:5 NKJV, is often inappropriately used in prayers of healing for the sick. In context, we see Isaiah 53:5-6 deals with our infirmities. The vicarious suffering of the Messiah heals our sin sickness, not our physical sickness.

In isolation, many in errantly use the scripture, *"Do not judge, or you too will be judged,"* from Matthew 7:1 as justification to sit back, ignore, and say and do nothing when they see wrong in the life of another believer. This is not congruent with other scripture regarding the accountability believers have for one another (Proverbs 27:17, Matthew 18:15-17). On the contrary, in context, the following verses in Matthew 7:2-5 call us to act—in order. Before we note and address our neighbor's issue (the speck in their eye), we are directed to first "judge" ourselves. Fix the wrong in us (remove the plank in our eye) so we may see more clearly and be able to help our neighbor fix their issue.

The context of scripture is so important that in *Understanding and Applying the Bible,* theologian Robertson McQuilkin asserts:

> *It is a shameful thing to carelessly ignore the context. To deliberately violate the context is more than shameful; it is sinful, for it is a deliberate substitution of one's own words for the Word of God. The student of Scripture, though he may not understand the original languages, nevertheless has at his command the*

single most important tool—the context. Let him use it diligently![23]

Now take it to the physical. Health and weight loss information is often presented in isolation. We get sound bites of a few craftily selected words that grab attention and don't tell the whole story. A look into the context adds needed clarity.

In isolation: The day after Thanksgiving on a TV shopping channel, I heard a guest say between Thanksgiving and New Year's, the average person gains 12 pounds. *Twelve pounds!* This was said several times with laughs, with verbal high fives with the show host, and follow-up statements about the inevitability of weight gain, "so why bother." First, her statement is not true. The average weight gain is significantly lower (one to two pounds).

But here is the context. The woman who touted the 12-pound holiday gain was selling jeans. Body-shaping jeans. Jeans with stretch. She encouraged viewers to eat up this season with the assurance that in her jeans, you will still look good and won't be uncomfortable. The "jeans sold" counter clicked up and up and up. Beyond the tens of thousands that bought the stretch jeans, millions took in that misinformation. *Pass the cookies!*

Biased information is sometimes obvious.

- The paleotarian will extol the virtues of meat-based eating.

- Vegans may try to lead you to believe meat will kill you.

- The weight watcher may say that counting and tracking is the key to weight loss.

- The person in bondage to food may assert that "life is short, we all have to die of something, so eat what/how much you want."

Other times, biases are not as clear. In these cases, follow the funding.

An example:

High-fructose corn syrup (HFCS) is made when corn starch is exposed to a series of enzymes and bacteria to convert some of the glucose modules to fructose. The resulting substance is cheaper than sugar, and HFCS 55 is sweeter than natural sugar. For these reasons, it is widely used by manufacturers in tons of products—primarily baked goods and soft drinks. HFCS is quickly absorbed by the body, and excess use has been linked to insulin resistance, type 2 diabetes, and weight gain.[24] Many nutritionists and medical professionals warn against its use.

SweetSurprise spreads "The Facts About High Fructose Corn Syrup," encouraging the public to "see through the media hype and get the facts to make healthy decisions."[25] Their website shares information to counter many of the negative health and obesity connections with HCFS. A series of SweetSurprise TV commercials assert that HFCS is "natural and like sugar is fine in moderation." Follow the funding. SweetSurprise.com is backed by the Corn Refiners Association (CRA), the national trade association representing the corn refining (wet milling) industry of the United States.

I started context checks on health and weight loss information after an unfortunate chocolate milk incident a few years ago. I enjoy chocolate and at the time, I was not averse to milk (had it in cereal and used it in cooking). So when news hit the health/fitness community that chocolate milk was a **perfect recovery** drink, my ears perked up. Chocolate milk has a carb-to-protein ratio (4 grams carbohydrate to 1 gram protein) that research has shown effectively replenishes glycogen stores and promotes muscle recovery needed after endurance exercise. This message was spread in running, fitness, and health magazines and websites. I saw it often on blog posts and in social media. Unchecked, this info was in my head.

Shortly thereafter at a marathon expo, I stopped by a chocolate milk booth. Reps gave out towels and shot video clips of runners stating how chocolate milk could fit into their recovery plan. Mind you, I'd never tried chocolate milk after a run, but I got the towel and on video talked about how chocolate milk is inexpensive, readily available, and as I periodically buy it for my son, it could be an easy fit to my recovery regimen. The next day after the marathon, the milk people were in the finisher chute, handing cold bottles to runners. I grabbed one, with sweaty hands ripped off the top and safety seal, and took a few gulps. Immediately, my body made it clear that chocolate milk was not wanted or needed at that moment. A friend who'd finished before me said he had the same reaction.

I got caught up by the dairy industry's effective marketing and took the chocolate milk message in isolation. I knew better than to try something new on race day, but I did it anyway. I didn't test my milk tolerance or listen to what my body needed at that moment. The carb-to-protein ratio of chocolate milk may be optimal, but its use is far from optimal for me. There are plenty of other recovery food/beverage options. I put aside things that worked for me to roll with something new that didn't.

I let information get me out of balance.

Step 3: Pray

Prayer keeps the balance.

Prayer guides towards truth.

Prayer helps us distinguish between what is good and what is best for us.

When prayer is neglected, we tend to lean on our own understanding.

When prayer becomes routine, we can fall into asking God to cosign decisions we have already made.

Thinking back, I didn't seek God's guidance **before** the chocolate milk recovery, my Master Cleanse attempt, or many other weight/fitness debacles on my record. But I sure got to praying when the consequences and frustration of the fail hit.

God can bless and direct our path. We have to seek Him first.

Am I suggesting we pray about our eating? Yes! Instead of asking God to bless our mess, we honor Him and benefit when seeking guidance on the choices before us.

The next sections outline foundations for healthy eating—steps for healthy weight maintenance I've settled on over time through research, observation, and personal experience. The concepts have been through filters of Berean behavior, content consideration, and prayer. These elements are part of my lifestyle, and I recommend them to my clients.

Every five years, the U.S. Department of Agriculture (USDA) and the U.S. Department of Health and Human Services (HHS) publish Dietary Guidelines for Americans. Based on a collective of substantiated nutrition science, the guidelines are designed to promote health and healthy weight maintenance and prevent chronic disease.

At the writing of this chapter (in December 2015), the 2015 Dietary Guidelines have not been released. The Scientific Report of the 2015 Dietary Guidelines Advisory Committee (DGAC) is used to direct the Dietary Guidelines. The DGAC provides a heads up on the direction of updated Dietary Guidelines. From the DGAC:

> *The overall body of evidence examined by the 2015 DGAC identifies that a healthy dietary pattern is higher in vegetables, fruits, whole grains, low- or non-fat dairy, seafood, legumes, and nuts; moderate in alcohol (among adults); lower in red and processed meat; and low in sugar-sweetened foods and drinks and refined grains.*[26]

This direction and my recommendations are aligned.

As you read the suggested foundations that follow, pray for guidance, check 'em out and evaluate to see what fits and can be effective for you.

Foundation 1 - Eat Less Meat

*Then God said, "I give you every seed-bearing plant on the
face of the whole earth and every tree that has fruit with
seed in it. They will be yours for food."*
Genesis 1:29

A perfectly prepared T-bone, strips of crispy bacon, fall-off-the-bone
ribs, smothered pork chops with rice and gravy or a plate of the
"gospel bird" (aka fried chicken)—for many, these options are the
start of some good eating.

We live in a meat and potatoes (or meat with rice and gravy)
culture. When describing a meal, most often the meat item is
mentioned first. It is the star of the meal, and other items on the plate
are back-up players.

Meat is a good source of protein; vitamins B12, B3 (niacin), and
B6; and the minerals iron and zinc. But too much of a good thing is
not good. Abundant studies connect high consumption of meat to
health risks. Here are just a few from recent health news:

- A National Cancer Institute study of 500,000 people
  found that those who ate the most red meat daily were 30
  percent more likely to die of any cause during a 10-year
  period than were those who ate the least amount of red
  meat.[27]

- Dr. Frank Hu led a Harvard School of Public Health long-
  term observational study of 120,000 men and women
  that "adds more evidence to the health risks of eating
  high amounts of red meat, which has been associated
  with type 2 diabetes, coronary heart disease, stroke, and
  certain cancers in other studies."[28]

- Carnitine (a nutrient in red meat) triggers a reaction in
  our digestive system that contributes to the narrowing or
  hardening of the arteries and the development of heart
  disease.[29]

- A recent study from the University of Texas MD
  Anderson Cancer Center substantiated a link between
  barbequed/grilled meat and kidney cancer. Grilling or
  pan-frying over high heat creates meat-cooking

mutagens, heterocyclic amines (HCAs) and polycyclic aromatic hydrocarbons (PAHs) that may increase the risk of renal cell carcinoma.[30]

- The World Health Organization reports several studies that "showed significant reductions in cancer risk among those who avoided meat. In contrast, Harvard studies showed that daily meat eaters have approximately three times the colon cancer risk, compared to those who rarely eat meat."[31]

- "An international panel of experts convened by the World Health Organization concluded eating processed meat like hot dogs, ham and bacon raises the risk of colon cancer and that consuming other red meats 'probably' raises the risk as well."[32]

Medical and nutritional discoveries are blessings. To whom much is given, much is required, and when we know better, we should do better. Yet, in spite of ample information about health risks, most Americans continue to eat too much meat. In 2012, the average American consumed 132 pounds of meat (75 pounds of red meat and 57 pounds of poultry). Calculations show average daily meat consumption is 71 percent higher than recommended for health in the 2010 Dietary Guidelines for Americans.[33]

Excess consumption of meat—particularly red meat—hinders health. To continue behavior shown and known to be harmful is poor physical stewardship.

Less meat is good for your health, your waistline, and the environment. We are called to be good stewards of all of God's creations, the earth as well as our bodies.

Did you know?

- The creation of one pound of beef requires 47 times more water than needed to grow one pound of vegetables.

- Livestock produces significantly more greenhouse gases than vegetable crops, and it takes 12 times more fossil fuel energy to produce one kilocalorie of animal protein than needed to make one kilocalorie of grain protein.

Food fed to the animals we eat could impact world hunger. "The meat industry uses so much energy to produce grain for livestock that if instead we used the grain to feed people following a vegetarian diet, it would be enough to feed about 840 million people."[34]

In the preface to *Old MacDonald's Factory Farm*, C. David Coats gives an interesting perspective:

> *Isn't man an amazing animal? He kills wildlife by the millions in order to protect his domestic animals and their feed. Then he kills domestic animals by the billions and eats them. This in turn kills man by the millions, because eating all those animals leads to degenerative—and fatal—health conditions like heart disease, kidney disease, and cancer. So then man tortures and kills millions more animals to look for cures for these diseases. Elsewhere, millions of other human beings are being killed by hunger and malnutrition because food they could eat is being used to fatten domestic animals.*[35]

All this considered and paired with three truths from scripture helped reframe my view of meat-based eating.

1. *[27]So God created mankind in his own image, in the image of God he created them; male and female he created them. [28]God blessed them and said to them, "Be fruitful and increase in number; fill the earth and subdue it. Rule over the fish in the sea and the birds in the sky and over every living creature that moves on the ground." [29]Then God said, "I give you every seed-bearing plant on the face of the whole earth and every tree that has fruit with seed in it. They will be yours for food." Genesis 1:27-29*

   When God created man and woman, humanity was vegetarian. Plants were our food. It was our original design. Note: Meat came on the scene as grub after the flood (Genesis 9:1-3).

2. *"I have the right to do anything," you say—but not everything is beneficial. "I have the right to do anything"—but not everything is constructive. 1 Corinthians 10:23*

   Just because I can do something doesn't mean that I should. Everything is not for me. God cares about what is best for me. I should as well.

3. *Show me the right path, O Lord;*
   point out the road for me to follow.
   Lead me by your truth and teach me,

for you are the God who saves me.
All day long I put my hope in you.
Psalm 25:4-5 NLT

The Lord knows the best path for me in all areas of my life.

This led me to the incorporation of Meatless Monday a few years ago. Currently I am a vegetarian. The removal of meat from my eating was not my plan; I was led to do so. After a fast, the Lord totally removed my taste for meat. I honored that leading and didn't force a return to my old pattern of eating. Since the change, I've settled at weight 15 pounds lighter, good blood pressure, cholesterol and glucose levels got better, my running pace improved by 30 seconds per mile—I even got a thigh gap. Moreover, my appreciation and enjoyment of natural, whole foods close to the way God put them here for us has expanded.

That said, I'm not anti-meat nor do I recommend everyone become a vegetarian. One pattern of eating does not fit all. I do, however, suggest (as research and general nutritional guidelines support), a look at the amount of meat consumed. If meals are meat based, reduce the amount and lean toward healthy sources of animal protein.

Meatless Monday and Meat on the Side are two simple ways to ease into healthy levels of meat consumption.

Meatless Monday

Meatless Monday is a nonprofit, international health initiative that encourages people to go meatless one day a week for personal health and the health of the planet. The movement has been adopted by schools, corporations, restaurants, and some communities across the globe.

The single step of skipping meat just one day per week reduces your overall meat consumption by 15 percent.

The transition to Meatless Monday was easy and welcomed by my meat-loving family. After a weekend of grab-and-go Saturday fare and our big breakfast and hearty supper on Sunday, the day of lighter, plant-based eating on Monday was a nice switch—a healthy jumpstart for the new week. Our family's finding was not unique. In an article published in the *American Journal of Preventive Medicine*, research on weekly rhythms and health considerations found 59 percent of people who start the week eating healthy find it easier to continue eating well the rest of the week.[36]

A day of meatless eating is not difficult. Consider these easy ideas:

Breakfasts	Lunches	Dinners	Snacks/Desserts
Oatmeal topped with fruit, nuts	Bean soup or minestrone and salad	Red beans and rice, green beans and cornbread	Nuts and dried fruit mix
Fortified cereal, almond milk, fruit	Veggie burger and fries	Vegetable stir fry, rice, veggie spring roll	Hummus and vegetable crudité or pita crisps
Grits, eggs, and toast with fruit	Vegetable supreme pizza, side salad	Vegetable lasagna, salad	Dark chocolate, peanut butter, tea
Omelet with vegetables and avocado toast	Grilled cheese and tomato soup	Vegetable plate - three favorite veggies with cornbread	Homemade apple crisp

For ideas, check out resources at meatlessmonday.com or follow my social media stream at nettyejohnson.com for meatless meal ideas every Monday. I'm always on the lookout for new eats. Tweet meal ideas using #MeatlessMonday to @nettyejohnson.

Meat on the Side

Meat on the Side flips the roles of meat and sides on the traditional American plate. Vegetables become the main theme of the plate, with meat as a side or seasoning.

With the rise of obesity and health risks connected to excess meat, progressive restaurateurs are adding entrees to their menus that use meat sparingly. In her *Wall Street Journal* "Food & Drink" column, Jane Black reports on the shift. She states, "Anchoring a plate with a massive hunk of animal protein is so last century." But not everyone wants a vegetarian plate. Meat on the side strikes a "balance between health and hedonism." The Culinary Institute of America's Menus of Change initiative teaches chefs to "make menus more healthful and sustainable, which in almost all cases means serving less meat."[37]

Meat on the Side doesn't require an upscale restaurant or a professional hand. It is easy to do. A simple example: Instead of two to three pieces of fried chicken, mashed potatoes with gravy, and a spoon of green peas, a fried chicken Meat on the Side flip may be a large salad with mixed greens and assorted vegetables topped with one piece of fried chicken sliced across the top and a delicious dressing. That's an easily accessible switch at home and listed at most American-style restaurants.

Another easy example for my home folks: In Louisiana, Monday means red beans. Often, red beans are cooked with pork and served with a four- to six-ounce hunk of andouille sausage. For Meat on the Side-style red beans, nix the cooking pork and use 10 to 12 ounces of sliced andouille sausage to season the whole pot of red beans. This significantly reduces the amount of meat (and saturated fat and nitrates) in the meal without sacrificing Creole flavor.

Meat on the Side reductions don't always require a change of cooking method or menu—just change what you put on your plate. Consider a breakfast with three slices of bacon, two eggs, some sausage, and grits or a biscuit. That meal has three high-fat protein sources (and no vegetables or fruit servings). Instead, select one meat to accompany the eggs (one whole egg, one egg white) and grits, and then add some fresh fruit and you have a skinnier, healthier, and more flavorful meal.

Meat on the Side can get deliciously creative. Check out Nikki Dinky at nikkidinkicooking.com for loads of finger-licking Meat on the Side recipes and meal ideas.

Common Questions and Concerns

If I reduce the amount of meat, how will I get the amount of protein needed?

Consult your medical professional for your specific protein requirements. Many people consume more protein than needed, so a reduction can bring levels into healthy guidelines. Additionally, reducing meat does not have to equal a reduction of protein intake. There are many plant-based protein sources that don't have the saturated fat and cholesterol of meat.

	Prot (g)	Cal	Chol (mg)	Sat Fat (g)
ANIMAL PROTEINS (COOKED)				
Chicken, dark meat (4 oz.)	27	270	155	5
Pork chop (4 oz.)	29	237	95	4
Ground beef, 80 lean (4 oz.)	27	279	95	7
Bacon (2 oz.)	20	311	61	8
Salmon (4 oz.)	28	173	62	1
Shrimp (4 oz.)	26	135	239	0.6
LEGUMES (cooked)				
Lentils (½ cup)	9	113	0	0.1
Black beans (½ cup)	8	114	0	0.1
Pinto beans (½ cup)	8	122	0	0.1
Red kidney beans (½ cup)	8	112	0	0.1
Black-eyed peas (½ cup)	8	110	0	0
Chickpeas (½ cup)	7	100	0	0.2

	Prot (g)	Cal	Chol (mg)	Sat Fat (g)
VEGETABLES (Cooked)				
Peas (½ cup)	5	67	0	0
Artichoke (1 med.)	4	64	0	0.1
Spinach (½ cup)	3	41	0	0.1
Mushrooms (1 cup)	5	15	0	0
Mustard greens (1 cup)	4	36	0	0
Green beans (1 cup)	2	44	0	0.1
GRAINS (Cooked)				
Wheat berries (½ cup)	6	107	0	0.1
Quinoa (½ cup)	4	111	0	0.2
Freekeh (½ cup)	6	130	0	0
Oatmeal (½ cup)	5	150	0	0.5
Brown rice (½ cup)	2	109	0	0.2
SEEDS AND NUTS				
Pumpkin seeds (1 oz.)	8	163	0	2.4
Flax seeds (1 Tbsp.)	2	55	0	0.4
Sunflower seeds (1 oz.)	5	165	0	1.5
Chia seeds (1 oz.)	5	138	0	1
Peanut butter (2 Tbsp.)	7	191	0	3
Almonds (1 oz.)	6	170	0	1
Pistachios (1 oz.)	6	161	0	1.6
Hazelnuts (1 ounce)	4	183	0	1.2
Walnuts (1 ounce)	4	180	0	1.5
Pecans (1 ounce)	3	201	0	1.8
OTHER				
Nutritional yeast (¼ cup)	8	60	0	0
Avocado (1 medium)	4	322	0	4
Vegetable burger (1 patty)	11	124	4	1

Prot = Protein, Cal = Calories, Chol = Cholesterol, Sat Fat = Saturated Fat

Sources: Sharon Palmer, *The Plant-Powered Diet* (New York: The Experiment, 2012), and USDA National Nutrient Database for Standard Reference

What meat sources are better for weight loss and general health?

Red meat (beef, pork, and lamb) tends to have significant amounts of cholesterol and saturated fats, which are linked to increased risk of heart disease. Processed meats like sausage, hot dogs, bacon, ham, and lunch meats, etc., often contain nitrates or nitrites that have been found to raise risk for certain cancers.

Poultry and seafood are better options with lower cholesterol and saturated fat than red meat. Additionally, omega-3 fatty acids in fish have been found to have heart health benefits.

Organic meat. To buy or not to buy?

When I think of where meat comes from, I picture my grandparents' beautiful farm, where the chickens ran free in their yard, the pigs wallowed in their pen and the cows roamed the large green pasture. They were fed grain-based feed and I never saw the administration of medication or drugs to the animals. This quaint memory of our family farm is not how most of the meat we eat is raised.

Conventionally raised livestock is business. Frequently animals are:

- raised in as little space as necessary (to maximize the number of animals)
- injected with antibiotics and hormones (to reduce loss and help them grow large and quickly)
- raised on feed that may have been exposed to pesticides or feed made from ground up animals (to keep costs low)

Some of the effects these conditions have on the animals are passed to those who eat the meat.

The USDA has strict standard for producers of organic meats. For example, to be certified organic, the livestock must have outdoor access, be fed certified organic feed, and no antibiotics or growth hormones can be used. The expense for these conditions is reflected in the higher cost of the product, but the result is a meat that is healthier and tastes better.

If it fits your budget, organic is a smart choice. Remember, if you are buying and eating less meat, the cost differential for organic may not be significant.

Examine Thyself

Is meat the star or supporting cast on your plate? Grab a pencil and sketch the proportions of meat, vegetables, fruit, and grains that were on your plate for yesterday's meals.

BREAKFAST

LUNCH

DINNER

Do you believe your weight and health could benefit from a reduction of meat?

❏ Yes ❏ No

If yes, list three benefits you would gain from this adjustment.

1. _____
2. _____
3. _____

Which method to reduce animal-based protein fits your preference and lifestyle?

❏ Meatless Monday ❏ Meat on the Side
❏ Both ❏ Other _____

Review the suggested meal ideas in the Meatless Monday chart on page 90. Circle any options that appeal to you. In the empty space on the chart, add other meatless breakfast, lunch, dinner, and snack items.

Revisit your artful renderings of yesterday's meals on pages 95 and 96. On the lines to the right of each picture, detail adjustments you could make to reduce meat and emphasize plant-based food.

Praction (Prayer - Action)

Journal your thoughts, prayer, and plan of action from this section.

Foundation 2 - Eat More Plants

Reducing the amount of meat on your plate makes space for nutrient-dense fruits and vegetables. This greatly benefits your weight and health.

The Mayo Clinic reports, "A plant-based diet, which emphasizes fruits, vegetables, grains, beans, legumes and nuts, is rich in fiber, vitamins and other nutrients. And people who eat only plant-based foods—aka vegetarians—generally eat fewer calories and less fat, weigh less, and have a lower risk of heart disease than nonvegetarians do.[38]

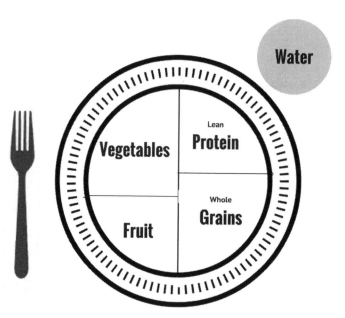

When it comes to fruits and vegetables, the more the better. The daily recommendation for adults is five combined servings of fruit and vegetables per day (approximately four to five cups). However, research shows in order to reap the full health benefits from fruits and vegetables, many adults need seven to 13 cups of produce per day.[39]

If you are a volume eater (meaning you need a larger amount of food to feel satisfied), this guideline works great for you. Fill up on fruits and vegetables.

If you don't like to eat a lot and this sounds like a lot of food, this guideline works great for you too. The guideline does not push you to eat beyond your comfort level. Just ensure that half of what you eat comprises fruits and vegetables.

Increasing the amount of plant-based food on your plate is not difficult. Regularly incorporate salads and roasted vegetables, and use fruit for sweets and treats.

Sensational Salads

Ever heard the saying, "A salad a day keeps extra pounds at bay"? *I thought I was being clever and made it up, but Google shows a few articles with similar phrasing.*

Giving salads a regular spot in your eating can aid weight loss, weight maintenance, and overall health. When mindfully made, salads are a convenient way to get multiple servings of fruits and vegetables. They are nutrient-dense meals providing vitamins, minerals, antioxidants, and fiber without a ton of calories. Most salads are quick, easy to prepare, versatile, portable, and plain delicious. I could eat a salad every day (and during warm months of the year, I typically do). The plate of greens with assorted veggie goodness fills me up, helps keep my systems working, and increases my appreciation of the bounty of tastes, textures and flavors God gave us. Plus, quickly throwing a delectable salad together makes me feel like a boss in the kitchen.

The key is to keep your healthy salad healthy.

My Salad Progression

Growing up, greens referred to turnips, mustards, or collards (from Daddy's garden), scrumptiously stewed with a pig part (hock or neck bone) and served with cornbread. Salad greens were not on the regular at our table. When we did have salad, it was fresh tomatoes and cucumbers (also from Daddy's garden) and iceberg lettuce I made limp with an overly generous dousing of Italian, French, or Thousand Island dressing. I thought I was doing something when I'd add cut-up lunch meat and American cheese. *I'm not the only one who has had a baloney and cheese salad!*

In the '80s, the salad bar in our dorm cafeteria and Wendy's Super Bar became my spots. This was also the beginning of my (misguided) good health efforts, so instead of a burger and fries, I'd go to the salad bar and load the plate with everything they had. Those salads were a sloppy, confused mess with a bunch flavors battling it out. Honestly, they were not too tasty and counting the nutritional costs of everything on it, I could have had a burger combo (and certainly would have enjoyed it more).

Thankfully, my experience with salad has evolved. Cookbooks, recipe blogs, great salads enjoyed in restaurants, and common sense have taught me that fresh is best and less is more. A bed of interesting greens or cruciferous vegetables tossed with a few fresh ingredients (that complement each other) and a simple vinaigrette is a beautiful thing. Instead of coating the palate, light simple salads keep the taste buds "clean," allowing us to truly taste the wonderful flavors God gave the ingredients.

The key is to stay mindful with salad making. Keep it simple to enjoy the natural flavors and protect the nutrient balance your body needs. Instead of recipes, I recommend a blueprint or ingredient guide to keep the salad tasty and healthy. Place your favorites on the list, then play.

Blueprint for a Sensational Seasonal Salad

My blueprint for simple seasonal salads involves a mix of dark salad greens (darker greens have more nutrients), a fresh seasonal fruit (for a punch of sweet flavor and vitamins), healthy nuts or seeds (healthy fat), and a bit of stinky cheese. Stinky cheese is my pet name for cheeses like blue cheese, goat cheese, and feta. These cheese varieties have bold flavors, so a small amount makes a big contribution to the dish. I sometime add this bit of indulgent fat for flavor and satiety.

Recipes are not needed; just select the veggie base, a fruit, nut, optional cheese, and accompanying dressing in line with what's fresh in the market or your kitchen. You can also throw in a lean protein or hearty grain to make it a stand-alone meal. The result is easy, delicious, nutritious, and economical.

Need ideas? Here are some of my go-to ingredients:

- **Favorite green/vegetable bases** – spinach, romaine, arugula, kale, or broccoli slaw (julienned broccoli stems). Most grocers now carry varieties of mixed greens that save time and are quite economical. I've been pleased with Organic Girl, Earthbound Farms, and Eat Smart brands.

- **Favorite fruit options** – Summer/Fall: tomatoes, strawberries, grapes. Winter/Spring: mandarin oranges, tangelos, sweet grapefruit, cherries, cranberries, Honeycrisp apples, Bosc pears.

- **Favorite nut/seed options** – pecans, almonds, walnuts, pumpkin seeds, sesame seeds. *Note: Lightly toasting nuts deepens the flavor. Carefully heat the nuts in a dry skillet over medium heat just until fragrant. Be careful not to overly brown or burn.*

- **Favorite stinky cheese options** – blue cheese, feta, goat cheese, parmesan, Asiago.

- **Favorite extras** – quinoa, black beans, lentils, or boiled egg for a heartier salad. Olives for added saltiness; dried cranberries for a touch of sweet; jalapeños or banana peppers for a kick of heat.

Dressings

To keep the salad healthy and slimming, skip creamy dressings. Thick dressings don't pour or spread easily, so you typically use larger amounts of dressing. This packs on the calories and saturated fat. For example, three tablespoons of ranch dressing can contain 210 calories and 24 grams of fat. That's 36 percent of the total daily recommended amount of fat in the salad dressing alone.

As an alternative, lightly flavor your selection of ingredients with a dressing homemade from olive oil, a flavored vinegar or mustard, and fresh herbs and seasonings. Comparatively, three tablespoons of a vinaigrette can contain 129 calories and 12 grams of fat.

Vinaigrette dressings also tend to be more flavorful and have a lower viscosity, so a smaller amount of dressing can be used to flavor a larger amount of vegetables. Making your own vinaigrette is simple: just put the ingredients in a Mason jar, screw on the lid, and shake. Toss the dressing and salad together and it is on!

Note: When only creamy dressing will do, stretch it. Instead of pouring dressing on the salad on your plate, place the salad ingredients in a bowl that has a lid. Pour a reasonable amount of dressing onto the greens. Pop on the top and shake the bowl like a maraca until all the greens are coated. The salad will look a bit beat up, but every bite will be deliciously dressed.

Roasted Vegetables

In my opinion, deep-frying and long simmering are crimes against vegetables.

Deep-frying can add calories. For example, according to the U.S. Department of Agriculture nutrition database,[40] a large (299 gram) baked potato contains 281 calories. A similarly sized serving of fried potatoes (308 grams) has a whopping 960 calories. *Are you sure you want fries with that?* Additionally, frying hides the flavor of the food. Fried foods pretty much taste the same.

With the exception of dried beans, long simmers reduce vegetables to bland mush. Texture and nutrition take a hit when we cook vegetables until they fall apart. Many vegetables have heat-sensitive nutrients that are damaged when the food is under heat for long periods of time. Water-soluble vitamins leach out into cooking water when vegetables are submerged for long periods of time. Southern-style green beans can be eaten with a spoon. They are "flavored" with pork and pork fat and cooked until they pretty much disintegrate. The result is creamy and salty. The God-given bright flavor and crisp texture of the green bean are cooked away.

In my opinion, roasting perfects the flavors of the vegetables. Instead of masking or diminishing the flavor, the notes are beautifully enhanced. Roast garlic and the strong, pungent flavor mellows to smooth, rich deliciousness. Roast yams, squash, corn, or beets and the natural sugars caramelize, adding a sweet, deep flavor. When roasted correctly, texture also benefits, producing crispy exteriors and soft insides.

Roasting a few sheet pans of vegetables on the weekend can bring bursts of flavor and nutrients to your meals all week long.

1. Hit your local farmer's market or produce stand for what looks good. Buy local and in season. Items will be fresher and less expensive, and following the cycle of the harvest adds variety.

2. Wash and prep the vegetables. Slice or dice according to density for uniform cooking.

3. Put vegetables in a bowl and add a bit of healthy oil. Olive and canola are my favorites. One to two tablespoons per sheet pan should be plenty. Don't add too much or the vegetables will be greasy.

4. Season with salt, pepper, and your favorite herbs. Toss until all vegetables are lightly coated.

5. Spread in a single layer on a baking sheet. Be sure not to crowd the pan or the veggies will steam instead of roast. Bake in an oven preheated to 425 degrees until fragrant and soft. Toss the vegetables halfway thru for even browning (about 15 to 20 minutes).

Roasted vegetables can be served as a delicious side. They are scrumptious as a stand-alone dish. Add a drizzle of balsamic reduction after you plate them and they will blow your mind.

Make a lot and refrigerate leftovers for use in breakfasts, lunches, and dinners the rest of the week. Some of my favorite uses include:

- **With eggs** – roasted veggies are amazing fillers for omelets, or stir them into whipped eggs/egg whites and bake in muffin tins for grab-and-go frittatas.

- **In soups** – bulk up canned or homemade soups. Add as you reheat the soup. The flavor and texture from roasting is a nice contrast from vegetables that are cooked in the soup.

- **Easy pilaf** – Mix roasted veggies with cooked brown rice, quinoa, freekeh, or other whole grains.

- **In a sandwich** – Pack the vegetables in a ciabatta roll with hummus and feta or between slices of focaccia with provolone and a flavored aioli.

- **In a naked burrito bowl** – Layer roasted vegetables, brown rice, black or pinto beans, and pico de gallo in a bowl. Top with salsa, guacamole, and cilantro.

- **In a wrap** – Toss roasted vegetables with mixed greens, nuts, and your favorite vinaigrette. Roll mixture in a whole wheat tortilla.

- **Over pasta** – Heat vegetables with pesto or marinara (or both), stir in whole-grain pasta of choice.

Options are endless.

Fruit

I'm sure you've heard "An apple a day keeps the doctor away." Fruit is a great source of vitamins, water, fiber, and other nutrients. Fruit is also a natural way to satisfy a sweet tooth with a lower amount of calories, fat, sodium, and preservatives than are present in other sweet treats (baked goods, candies, ice creams, etc.). *As always, if you have diabetes or any other medical condition with specific dietary concerns, consult your medical professional.*

Train your brain to seek out fruit for snacks and desserts and use fruit as a sweetener. For example, instead of sugar, add sliced fruit or berries to tea or use a sliced banana instead of jelly on your next PB&J sandwich. *I understand Elvis loved peanut butter and banana sandwiches. I think they are mighty tasty as well—thank you very much. (I couldn't resist!)*

Out of sight is out of mind. Use visual cues to your advantage. Get the day's servings of fruits and vegetables out of the bins or the refrigerator. Place a bowl of seasonal fruit or an attractive plate of vegetable crudité in easy reach for snacking or nibbling during your day. Reach for them instead of crackers, chips, cookies, or mints.

Common Questions and Concerns

Fruit and vegetables are expensive!

This common belief is not always true. In general, produce is less expensive than meat. Legumes (beans) are pennies per serving and canned vegetables are often less than a buck.

The key for cost-effective produce is buying whole items, buying local and in season, and buying on sale.

- **Whole items.** Fresh prewashed, precut, and prepackaged means premium pricing. You are paying for convenience. It takes very little time to wash and cut fruits and vegetables. When offered, buy fresh produce whole and dirty and wash it as you use it. This will save money and help preserve the freshness of the produce. (*Many wash and prep produce as soon as they buy it. Bacteria can grow on stored washed vegetables in the refrigerator. Additionally, wet produce will spoil faster. It is best to wash fruit and vegetables right before you prepare or eat it.*)

- **In season.** When produce is out of season, it has to travel from another part of the world to your market. This long-distance travel needs to happen fast to prevent spoilage. That is expensive. When food is in season, it can be grown locally, or at least closer by. In-season produce is less expensive and often much more flavorful.

- **Buy local.** Regularly visit your local farmer's market where growers in the area bring their harvest for sale. This bypasses the middleman, so pricing is spectacular. The produce is super-fresh (often picked the day before market). It is also a wonderful opportunity to get to know the growers and support your local economy.

- **On sale.** If cost is a concern, always shop sales. Check the weekly circulars for the produce loss leaders (items sold at a very low price to get you in the store). Also look for unadvertised sales. Produce is perishable. Grocers don't want to throw food out. I often check with the produce manager and purchase ripe items at half price when I know I will eat or cook it that day. (Notice I said ripe, not rotten!)

Fresh, canned, or frozen. Which is better?

Fresh is not always best. The moment a fruit or vegetable is picked, decomposition begins. "Fresh" produce in the grocery store could have been picked many days ago. Some produce is picked well before it is ripe so it will survive the transport timing. (Buying fresh local does away with this problem.)

Frozen produce is frozen shortly after it is picked. This halts the decomposition process. Hence frozen foods often have more nutrients than grocery fresh produce.

Canned produce is also typically processed shortly after harvest. As with freezing, nutrients are locked in. The drawback with canned produce lies in the high amount of sodium added in the process and bisphenol A (BPA) in some can linings that leaches into the food product. Choose canned goods in BPA-free cans and peep at the label for sodium levels.

What about organic produce? Does it make a difference?

Concern about pesticides used on crops is valid. Chemicals are widely used to control weeds, insects, rodents, and even fungus and bacteria that attack crops. We don't want this in our bodies. The Environmental Working Group (EWG) compiled data from pesticide tests on produce for a decade. From this data came two lists: the Dirty Dozen and the Clean Fifteen. Dirty Dozen foods have the highest pesticide load. Go organic with these whenever you can. The Clean Fifteen have the lowest pesticide load. Purchasing conventionally grown version of these foods is okay.

Dirty Dozen (Buy Organic)	Clean Fifteen (Buy Conventional)	
Apples	Avocados	Papayas
Strawberries	Sweet corn	Kiwi
Grapes	Pineapples	Eggplant
Celery	Cabbage	Grapefruit
Peaches	Sweet peas (frozen)	Cantaloupe (domestic)
Spinach	Onions	Cauliflower
Sweet bell peppers	Asparagus	Sweet potatoes
Nectarines (imported)	Mangoes	
Cucumbers		
Cherry tomatoes		
Snap peas (imported)		
Potatoes		

Recipe: Banana "Ice Cream"

Makes 1 serving (1 to 1 ½ cups)
This dairy-free, fat-free, no-added-sugar, one-ingredient, creamy
dreamy dessert couldn't be easier.

Ingredients:

2-3 ripe bananas

Instructions:

Peel and slice ripe bananas into 1-inch chunks. Place in Ziploc bag and freeze until hard.

Place frozen banana chunks in Vitamix or other high-quality blender and pulse to break the chunks into pieces.

Blend using the tamper to push the mixture into the blades and your patience to keep at it until creamy. It may not look like it, but the mixture will come together to resemble soft-serve ice cream. If not using a Vitamix, stop the blender periodically and using a spatula, scrape down the sides.

When smooth and creamy, you have your banana base. Enjoy as is or hook it up with your favorite add-ins. Here are some tried and true combos.

Mix in	And you'll get
Peanut butter	Peanut butter banana "ice cream"
Nutella	Hazelnut banana "ice cream"
Frozen strawberries	Strawberry banana "ice cream"
Chopped cacao nips	Chocolate chip banana "ice cream"
Maple syrup, chopped cacao nips, and chopped walnuts, a pinch of salt	Maple walnut banana "ice cream"

Examine Thyself

Using the scale of 1 to 5 below, rate your current intake of fruit and vegetables.

1	2	3	4	5

| Do french fries count? | | I eat fruit & vegetables when I can. | | Bring 'em on. I luv the Veggie Life! |

List three benefits of increasing fruit and vegetable intake in your eating.

1. _____

2. _____

3. _____

10 fruits and vegetables you currently eat and enjoy	3 fruits or vegetables you will try in the next 30 days

Praction (Prayer - Action)

Journal your thoughts, prayer, and plan of action from this section.

Foundation 3 - Limit Refined Sugar[41]

Refined sugar starts with a plant—corn, rice, sugar cane, sugar beets, etc. The whole food item is processed. Minerals, vitamins, fiber, water, and other nutritionally beneficial components are stripped away to extract and concentrate its pure sweetness. What remains are empty calories—naked carbohydrates in that sweet granule or syrup many of us love and consume too much of.

Americans eat an estimated 130 to 150 pounds of sugar per year—yes, I said 130 to 150 pounds! Most of it is hidden in packaged goods. Food manufacturers add refined sugars to almost everything. Of course, sugar is prevalent in sugary drinks, candies, ice cream, cookies, cakes, and other sweet goods. But don't blame it all on the donuts and sweet tea. Sugar is also added to commercially produced savory items like breads, crackers, salad dressings, marinades, and pasta sauce. As a matter of fact, 74 percent of packaged foods sold in grocery stores contains added sugar.

Excessive sugar can make us fat and sick. Studies link excessive sugar to the development of cardiovascular disease (the number one cause of death in the United States), hypertension, fatty liver disease, kidney disease, obesity, and type 2 diabetes.

Sugar also negatively affects our brain. Endocrinologist Dr. Medha Munshi cites mounting research that "offers more evidence that the brain is a target organ for damage by high blood sugar."[42] Chronically high sugar levels are linked to increased incidences of depression, increased risk of the development of Alzheimer's, and reduced memory, mental processing, and learning abilities.

Conflict and discussion are ongoing about the toxicity and addictive properties of sugar. Dr. William Coda Martin classified refined sugar as a poison and Dr. Mark Hyman, Director of the Cleveland Clinic for Functional Medicine, states that "the science demonstrating that people can be biologically addicted to sugar in the same way we can be addicted to heroin, cocaine or nicotine is clear."[43]

What is also clear, for the average American, is that a reduction of added sugar in the diet is essential for good health.

How much is optimal?

The 2010 USDA Dietary Guidelines for Americans do not provide a clear sugar intake recommendation. These guidelines recommend that calories for added sugar and trans fats combined not exceed 5 to 15 percent of the total daily caloric intake. While not yet released, recommendations for the 2015 Dietary Guidelines are to cap added sugar to 10 percent of the daily diet.

The most definitive guideline for the general public comes from the American Heart Association (AHA). Due to excess sugar's connection to heart disease, the AHA "recommends limiting the amount of added sugars you consume to no more than half of your daily discretionary calories allowance. For most American women, that's no more than 100 calories per day, or about 6 teaspoons of sugar. For men, it's 150 calories per day, or about 9 teaspoons."[44] *Note: As always, if you have a medical condition, the recommendation for you is best determined by your doctor or other healthcare professional.*

For many, a reduction to levels recommended for good health is significant. How do you get there?

A Google search for sugar detox returned over 5 million results. A search for tips to reduce sugar yielded 22 million. I'll briefly outline three.

- **Cold Turkey** – *The Blood Sugar Solution 10-Day Detox Diet* by Dr. Mark Hyman is a popular program designed to break sugar and carb cravings. The method uses a cold turkey approach, as he asserts, "There is no way to handle a true physiological addiction except to stop it completely." Over a 10-day period, you remove all forms of sugar, flour products, and artificial sweeteners from your eating and follow 10 Big Ideas to automatically reset your body's neurotransmitters and hormones.

This method may be a good fit for people with a strong will and desire to break a strong sugar addiction. It is stringent, with no sweets. Focus and follow-through are required.

- **Phased Approach** – In her book *52 Days: Countdown to Your Best Body*, registered dietician Sohailla Digsby uses a phased approach to sugar reduction. The program begins with a daily limit of five grams of added sugar per day. Over the course of 52 days, it increases to 10 grams of added sugar per day and ends at 25 added sugar grams per day—a healthy and hopefully livable level. A challenge with this method is accurate identification of added sugar (refined/processed) vs. natural sugar (sugar in milk, or lactose; sugar in fruit, or fructose, etc.). The USDA does not require manufacturers to distinguish naturally occurring sugars from refined or added sugars.

This approach may be a good fit for detail-oriented individuals who want to enjoy refined sugar in moderation. Reading the nutrition labels of foods and counting and tracking the number of sugar grams in food takes time and commitment.

- **Natural + Moderation Method** – This method includes sugar from natural sources (fruit, honey, maple syrup, etc.). You get the sweet without the junk. Natural sugars typically contain fewer chemicals and more nutritive elements, that is, fiber, vitamins, minerals, antioxidants, and so forth. Some natural sugar sources (for example, honey or maple syrup) also have flavor profiles that can cause people to use less naturally.

With this method, you get sweet but no refined sugar. No tracking or counting is involved, just examination of ingredient lists on processed foods to scope out added sweeteners. This method may be a fit for those who want sweets from natural sources. Keep in mind, just because the sugar is natural, it is still sugar. When eating natural sweets, listen to your body and the Holy Spirit to know when you have had enough.

If you find honey, eat just enough—too much of it, and you will vomit. Proverbs 25:16 NIV

Whatever method you choose, reduction is important. The more sugar you consume, the more your body will crave.

Sneaky Sources of Added Sugar

Reducing sugar can be tricky because we have to tune in to its presence. Sugar is frequently added to items that don't taste sweet. Even though we don't notice the sweet flavor, our body responds to it. Sugar has dozens of aliases. Following is a list of names for sugar that appear on product labels:[45]

Agave nectar	Demerara sugar	Maltol
Barbados sugar	Dextrin	Maltose
Barley malt	Dextrose	Mannose
Barley malt syrup	Evaporated cane juice	Maple syrup
Beet sugar	Free-flowing brown	Molasses
Brown sugar	sugars	Muscovado
Buttered syrup	Fructose	Palm sugar
Cane juice	Fruit juice	Panocha
Cane juice crystals	Fruit juice concentrate	Powdered sugar
Cane sugar	Glucose	Raw sugar
Caramel	Glucose solids	Refiner's syrup
Carob syrup	Golden sugar	Rice syrup
Castor sugar	Golden syrup	Saccharose
Coconut palm sugar	Grape sugar	Sorghum syrup
Coconut sugar	HFCS (High-fructose	Sucrose
Confectioner's sugar	corn syrup)	Sugar (granulated)
Corn sweetener	Honey	Sweet sorghum
Corn syrup	Icing sugar	Syrup
Corn syrup solids	Invert sugar	Treacle
Date sugar	Malt syrup	Turbinado sugar
Dehydrated cane juice	Maltodextrin	Yellow sugar

I have sweet teeth (i.e., a sweet tooth x 32). The Natural + Moderation Method works best for me and I often recommend it to my clients. Natural sweeteners satisfy my taste for sweet but don't cause the cravings or over indulgences that occur when I consume significant amounts of refined sugar. Periodically, I will have a food with refined sugar, but my primary sources of sweet are fruit, honey, and maple syrup.

Dates – The fruit of a palm tree provides my favorite and most frequently used natural sweetener. Dried dates are super-sweet with a delicious, caramel-like flavor. They also contain vitamin B6 and potassium, copper, manganese, and magnesium. I throw a few dates in the blender to sweeten smoothies or add chopped dates into the cooking water to sweeten oatmeal and other cooked breakfast cereals. I also use date butter (also called date paste) to add sweetness and flavor to baked goods or as a jelly-like spread on toast or sandwiches. It is simple to make—lightly simmer the dates in an equal amount of water until the fruit softens. Cool, remove the pits, and pulverize in a food processor (adding cooking water) until smooth. The caramelly sweet spread will hold for about a week in the refrigerator. I also use a large variety of fruit for sweeteners. Apples and applesauce, smashed bananas, pineapple, raisins, prunes, dried cherries, dried apricot and apple juice-infused dried cranberries as well as assorted frozen fruits are excellent natural sweeteners. In addition to sweetness, they each add their own unique flavor, fiber, moisture, vitamins, and other helpful nutrients.

Honey – I enjoy the light floral flavor of honey and use it as a sweetener in drinks, hot and cold cereals, homemade granola and energy bars, and smoothies. Honey is also fantastic instead of sugar in baked goods (cornbread and biscuits), and a peanut butter and honey sandwich is killer. Note: Honey is a natural product that may contain Clostridium botulinum spores that are harmful to the immature digestive systems of babies. Never give honey or homemade foods with honey to children under the age of one.

Maple syrup – Maple syrup is boiled xylen sap of the maple tree. I prefer Grade B Maple syrup, which is dark and more intensely flavored. In addition to the delicious maple-y flavor, this syrup has good amounts of zinc and manganese. I use it regularly in baked goods and in dishes made with fall vegetables.

Examine Thyself

Do sweets pose a challenge for your weight and healthy eating? If not, then go you! If they do, list three benefits you could gain from reducing the amount of refined sugar.

1. _____
2. _____
3. _____

A quick win is a change that relatively easy to make that progresses you toward your goal. Prayerfully review your eating habits and list one to three quick wins related to sugar. Pick one and adopt the change and repeat. When it becomes habit, go to the next on the list. Rack up some wins.

1. _____
2. _____
3. _____

Sweets are often connected to experiences (for example, cake is associated with birthday celebrations and weddings; cookies are viewed as a reward; chocolate is a stress reliever; and so on). If you have these connections, complete the table below with relations that pose a challenge.

Event or Experience	Automatic Sugar Response	Other Possible Responses

Praction (Prayer - Action)

Journal your thoughts, prayer, and plan of action from this section.

Foundation 4 - Water, Water, Water

Our bodies are 60 percent water, and drinking enough water has many health benefits.

- **Drinking water helps keep body fluid levels in check.** Digestion, blood circulation, the transportation of nutrients, regulation of body temperature, and other critical bodily functions rely on adequate hydration.

- **Water can help you lose weight.** Often we confuse thirst for hunger and give solid food (and extra calories) to the body's call for liquid. Drinking a glass of water before eating meals has been scientifically proven to cause you to eat less and thus lose weight.

- **Water helps your kidneys.** The kidneys filter the blood, excreting waste, toxins, and excess fluid through urine. Adequate water is needed for this process.

- **Water can help keep your heart healthy.** When not adequately hydrated, vital organs pull water from blood. This increases the blood's viscosity (makes it thicker), which causes the heart to work harder to circulate blood.

- **Water helps keep you regular.** When not enough water is present, the body will also pull fluid from stool in the intestines. The result—constipation. Constipation is not fun.

- **Water helps keep skin looking good.** When dehydrated, our skin looks dry, ashy, and wrinkly. Dry, ashy, and wrinkly is not attractive.

How much water is enough?

For years, we have heard that everyone needs eight 8-ounce glasses of water per day. It is not clear how that guideline was established, and there is no research that supports a single amount for all people. Many personal and environmental factors come into play, including the amount of exercise, temperature, humidity, illness, and others.

The Institute of Medicine offers gender-based recommendations of about three liters (about 13 cups) for men and approximately 2.2 liters (about nine cups) for women a day.

The University of California, Irvine uses body weight as a guideline. To calculate appropriate daily consumption, divide your weight by two. The resulting quotient is an estimate of how much fluid your body requires each day in ounces. For example, a 160-pound person would need 80 ounces (10 eight-ounce glasses).

The bottom line is that you want to take in enough to stay adequately hydrated. If signs of dehydration appear (for example, dry or sticky mouth, reduced tear production, dry skin, reduced urine production, or urine that has a strong smell or deep color), drink up.

If drinking water is not a habit, these tips can help:

- Each night, put a glass or small bottle of water on your nightstand. While you may not feel thirsty, water levels are low in the morning. Overnight, perspiration, the creation of urine, and evaporation from breathing takes water from your system. Drink up before you get out of bed to revive your body.

- Sip while you are at the sink taking care of morning hygiene tasks and primping to make yourself pretty (or handsome).

- Drink a glass of water before breakfast.

- Keep a bottle of water with you (in your car, on your desk at the office). Set triggers to sip. (*When someone driving you crazy makes you want to ... bless them, take a sip. Each time you check Facebook, take a sip. Each time your phone rings, take a sip.*). Make it fun.

- Drink a glass of water before lunch.

- Feeling the midday slump? Instead of grabbing a coffee, candy bar, or bag of chips, drink a glass of water and walk around, stretch, do a few push-ups, or put on an upbeat gospel song and vigorously sing. Water and something that gets your body moving will do wonders for your energy.

- Drink a glass of water before your dinner meal.

- If you exercise during the day *(or should I say **when** you exercise ...)* drink before and after.

See how easy it can be to get your water?

In her Drink Up initiative, First Lady Michelle Obama encourages people, saying, "It's really that simple. Drink just one more glass of water a day and you can make a real difference for your health, your energy, and the way you feel. So Drink Up and see for yourself."[46]

Yes, this will cause frequent trips to the bathroom. This is a good thing. Remember, wastes and toxins are released in urine. Get it out!

A word about water bottles: I count a nice water bottle as a must-have tool for weight loss, fitness, and health. Out of sight, out of mind. Keeping water with you means you will drink more water—and it helps you drink fewer sugary drinks.

Forgo the disposable water bottles. It wastes money, is horrible for the environment, and is not the best for your body. Ban the Bottle estimates that Americans use about 50 billion plastic water bottles in a year. Less than one-fourth of them were recycled. Additionally, some plastics used in bottles are hazardous to your health.

The next time you put a plastic bottle to your mouth or eat food from a container, check the recycling symbol on the bottom. The arrowed triangle surrounds a number that identifies the plastic used.

Code	Plastic	Information/Considerations
1	PET/PETE Polyethylene Terephthalate	Thin plastic used in clear water bottles. Use only one time. Not recommended that you heat or refill the bottle.
2	HDPE High-Density Polyethylene	Thick opaque plastic often used in toys, detergent bottles, and milk jugs. Safe to reuse.

Code	Plastic	Information/Considerations
3	V Polyvinyl Chloride	Substantial plastic used in squeeze bottles. Contains phthalates which are linked to cancer. DO NOT USE.
4	LDPE Low-Density Polyethylene	Flexible thin plastic used in grocery store, shopping, dry cleaning, and garbage bags. Also used in plastic wrap.
5	PP Polypropylene	For straws, syrup bottles, yogurt bottles.
6	PS Polystyrene	Hard, rigid plastic used in plastic silverware and foam tray and cups. Leaches neurotoxin styrene. DO NOT USE.
7	Other	Used in clear plastic silverware, food can linings. Often contains BPA. DO NOT USE.

Information source: Race Against Chemicals in the Environment

Norex Movement offers this rhyme to remembers which plastics are safe "1, 2, 5, 4: These are the ones you're looking for!" Stay away from the others.

I have and recommend glass bottles. Glass is safer. There are no leaching chemicals, and glass bottles can be cleaned and sterilized. *Plastic bottles get stained and ooky.* Concerned about breakage? Many styles have stylish protective silicone covers. *Kind of like an OtterBox for your water bottle.*

Common Questions and Concerns

What about soft drinks? Don't they count as water?

Yes, and in my opinion, no. Yes, they are a liquid. But they have stuff in them. A lot of stuff in them. Soft drinks contain sweeteners. Ridiculous amounts of sugar. Truly visualize this. Go to the kitchen, get a pretty glass and spoon in 10 teaspoons of sugar. Would you pick up that glass and kick it back? Of course not! That is in no way attractive or tolerable. The soda industry makes it so. (An average 12-ounce soda contains 10.2 teaspoons of sugar.) They include artificial flavors, carbonation, sodium, and sometimes a bit of caffeine, so we will drink it up and serve it to our children.

But I do diet soda.

It still has sweetener. Chemical artificial sweetener replaces the sugar or high-fructose corn syrup used in regular soda. Still not good.

Here's the thing. Water gives our bodies the fluid it needs with no calories or health-harming ingredients. Soft drinks give us fluid our bodies need and flavor we want. The rest is not good. As it relates to weight loss, a 10-year study from the University of Texas found that those who drank two or more diet soft drinks a day had a 500 percent greater increase in waist circumference than those who did not drink sodas.[47] A 500 percent greater increase in belly measurement, and this was with diet (calorie-free) soda! Researchers believe this huge difference is partially due to the way sweeteners in soft drinks confuse the body. They also suspect a psychological factor. ("I had a diet soft drink—so I'll take the biggie fry" kind of thing).

But I don't like the taste of water.

I understand, as I hear this often. But I'm also challenged to understand this. True, hard water or water with impurities can have an off taste. In that case, get a water filter. No one likes water with contaminants.

But clean water. To not like the taste of clean water is akin to not liking the smell of fresh air. The question becomes, how did this dislike develop? It is possible that water is distasteful because the taste buds have become accustomed to added flavors in drinks. Here's the good news—taste buds are somewhat fickle. If they can't be with the one they love, they learn to love the one they're with. Continued exposure to soft drinks or juices or the chemicals and artificial flavorings in those water mix-in packets will deepen the dependence on the flavors. Flip it. Drink more water and the taste buds will adjust. Water will become tolerable. You may come to love it. If you just have to have some flavor, make citrus water by slicing some orange, lemon, or lime in the water. Or make a berry water by infusing it with fruit. You can make it work.

Examine Thyself

Using gender guidelines or the weight based recommendation on page 119, how much water should you get per day?

_____

Do you reach this amount? ❑ Yes, everyday ❑ Sometimes ❑ Nope

If your intake is below the recommended amount, list three benefits you could gain from increasing your water consumption.

1. _____

2. _____

3. _____

Praction (Prayer - Action)

Journal your thoughts, prayer, and plan of action from this section.

Foundation 5 - Sleep

This may be a mommy thing, but seeing my babies (well ... anyone's babies) in peaceful slumber touches my heart.

They look so precious and peaceful, and I admire how most little ones embrace sleep. When it calls—regardless of where or when—they answer. It's great that they do. That time of still, calm inactivity has a lot going on that is essential to good health.

The ability to sleep well is an important skill. Are you a good sleeper?

Most of us know how the lack of sleep negatively affects our energy and appearance. It can hinder our cognitive performance and push us to lean towards cranky. But did you know that lack of sleep can affect your body fat?

A University of Chicago study compared two groups of dieters. One group got adequate sleep; the other group was sleep deprived. While both groups lost similar amounts of weight, more than half of the pounds lost by the well-rested group were body fat. The sleepy group lost more muscle mass. This is not good!

The sleepy group also reported being hungry. David Rapoport, MD, director of the NYU Sleep Disorders Program, states, "When you are sleepy, certain hormones go up in your blood, and those same hormones drive appetite."

It gets worse. Did you know that lack of sleep may also increase your risk of death?

Research published in the *European Heart Journal* reports that a chronic lack of sleep (defined as less than six hours per night—oy!) raised the risk of developing or dying from heart disease by 48 percent and stroke by 15 percent![48]

"When you're sleeping you're regulating hormone levels, you're regulating insulin levels, your blood pressure is being kept under control, there are a lot of things going on, and if you're not getting enough sleep you're throwing these things out of whack," says Shelby Freedman Harris, PsyD, director of behavioral sleep medicine at

Montefiore Medical Centers Sleep-Wake Disorders Center in New York City.[49]

How much sleep is optimal?

Adults need at least seven, but no more than nine hours of sleep at night to aid with the prevention of heart disease. Seven to nine hours not happening? The National Sleep Foundation recommendations include the following tips for a full night of restorative sleep:[50]

- **Be active.** Daily exercise can greatly enhance the amount and quality of sleep at night. Take note of the time for your exercise. For some, exercising early in the day is best, since a workout close to bedtime makes falling asleep difficult.

- **Be regular.** Go to bed and wake up at the same time. (Yes, this includes weekends.) The regularity of schedule helps set your sleep cycle.

- **Be predictable.** Think back to your childhood bedtime routine. Bath time, brush teeth, lay out next day's clothes, story time or reading, prayers, lights out ... The elements of that routine helped you wind down and told your body it was time to go to sleep. Set up a bedtime routine with relaxing "unplugged" tasks that allow your body and mind to slow down before you hit the sheets.

- **Be comfortable.** Speaking of sheets—set up your bedroom to support rest. Sleep experts recommend a cool temperature (between 60 and 67 degrees). Outfit your bed with comfortable sheets, pillows and an appropriately supportive mattress. Cut off electronics and eliminate light and distracting noises.

- **Be aware of sleep-disrupting substances.** The consumption of alcohol, caffeine, nicotine, and spicy foods close to bedtime can hinder your rest. If you indulge in these items, do so earlier in the day to keep sleep happy.

The Word of God gives us this beautiful encouragement for trouble sleeping.

Not sleeping from too much work?

> *It is in vain that you rise up early*
> *and go late to rest,*
> *eating the bread of anxious toil;*
> *for he gives to his beloved sleep.*

Psalm 127:2 ESV

Not sleeping because you are fearful about something or worried?

> *You can go to bed without fear;*
> *you will lie down and sleep soundly.*

Proverbs 3:24 NLT

> *Things not going well and it keeps you up at night?*
>
> *⁶Many people say, "Who will show us better times?"*
> *Let your face smile on us, Lord.*
>
> *⁷You have given me greater joy*
> *than those who have abundant harvests of grain and new wine.*
> *⁸In peace I will lie down and sleep,*
>
> *for you alone, O Lord, will keep me safe.*

Psalm 4:6-8 NLT

Anything on your mind or heart disrupting rest? Give it to God. He can handle it.

Examine Thyself

For the next week, complete the following sleep log. Record the date, the number of hours you slept, your thoughts before laying your head down to rest, and what is on your heart and mind when you wake.

Date: Hours Sleep: Quality of Rest:	Thoughts before sleep:	Thoughts upon waking:
Date: Hours Sleep: Quality of Rest	Thoughts before sleep:	Thoughts upon waking:

| Date:

Hours
Sleep:

Quality
of Rest:	Thoughts before sleep:	Thoughts upon waking:
Date:

Hours
Sleep:

Quality
of Rest: | Thoughts before sleep: | Thoughts upon waking: |

Date: Hours Sleep: Quality of Rest:	Thoughts before sleep:	Thoughts upon waking:
Date: Hours Sleep: Quality of Rest:	Thoughts before sleep:	Thoughts upon waking:

Date: Hours Sleep: Quality of Rest:	Thoughts before sleep:	Thoughts upon waking:

Notes on this week's sleep:

Praction (Prayer - Action)

Journal your thoughts, prayer, and plan of action from this section.

CHAPTER 6

Adopt a Food Philosophy

If you don't know what you stand for, you will fall for anything.
Unknown

FOR THE PAST FEW decades, mission statements have been extremely popular. They are a collection of statements that succinctly define the values and objectives of an organization or individual. A mission statement is a credo or philosophy used to guide thought and action. It is an informing statement to others and a reminder to self of who you are, what you do, and what you believe to be important.

Large corporations invest significant amounts of time and resources to the creation and communication of their mission. Most successful social and civic organizations have mission statements. I've even come across families that have value statements they use as tools for discussion, problem solving, and decision-making.

Many years ago, I was involved with the ministry team that formulated the mission and vision statement for my home church. The process took months. For background, we unpacked the purpose of the universal church and the local church. We married that general purpose with the specific purpose, functioning, and the visionary goals from our pastor. We prayerfully reviewed and reworked the wording until the statement was finalized and approved. To this day, the mission statement is recited at the beginning of every worship, teaching, outreach event, or meeting at the church. The verbal utterance of who we are, whose we are, and what we are called to do sets the focus for what is about to happen.

One of the most ardent aspects of starting my business was the definition of my organization's mission. I did a lot of talking to God and talking to myself to capture in words the organization's reason for being. This investment of time has proven to be fruitful. Whenever an idea or opportunity presents itself, I take a moment to consider if and how it aligns with my mission. It is a wonderful reminder that not everything that looks good is necessarily good for the business. No matter how attractive, if it does not progress our purpose, values, or beliefs, I take a pass.

The application of a mission or value tool is powerful for health goals. A succinct definition of elements key to your healthy weight management clears clutter and makes it easier to make good choices. A few examples:

Two thousand years ago Hippocrates outlined a health standard in his statement, "If we could give every individual the right amount of nourishment and exercise, not too little and not too much, we would have the safest way to health."

Contemporary food researcher and author Michael Pollan boils healthy eating down to seven words: "Eat Food. Mostly Plants. Not Too Much."[51]

Statements to focus and guide eating are also contained in scripture. One of my favorites was penned by the apostle Paul:

[23]*"I have the right to do anything," you say—but not everything is beneficial. "I have the right to do anything"—but not everything is constructive.* [31]*So whether you eat or drink or whatever you do, do it all for the glory of God.* 1 Corinthians 10:23, 31

Notice the wisdom and guidance in these simple statements. Hippocrates points to the importance of nutritional value, portion control, and exercise. Michael Pollan's words guide us towards real, whole food, plant-based eating, and portion control. Paul, in his writing about the freedom we have in Christ reminds that just because we *can* have something doesn't mean that we *should* have that something. We must consider how and whom it benefits. Everything we do (including what we eat) should be done for the glory of God.

This is truth. Powerful truth!

Imagine the change when value statements such as these are believed to be true, and checked before choices are made and actions are taken.

Now, move past imagining and apply this principle to eating.

My Food Philosophy

Several years ago, I developed a mission statement of sorts regarding my eating. I call it my Faithfully Fit Food Philosophy. Like the creation of the mission statement at church and for my company, this process took a considerable amount of time, thought, and prayer. Finding the elements that are important and impactful to my health and weight management took some digging.

God blessed the effort and intent. My behaviors change dramatically when I quickly visit the statement *before* making a food selection. I can't tell you the number of times I've picked up fruit instead of a pastry at a morning meeting or pulled out of the drive-thru line when my food philosophy crossed my mind.

The beautiful part is how easy healthy decision-making becomes. It is like shining a light in a dark place. Decisions are made clearer and attractive. With repetition, the choices become habits and part of your new and improved lifestyle.

For this reason, I advise my clients to adopt their own food philosophy and beloved, I invite you to do the same. Create a collection of food-related statements that support your values and weight management success.

For a framework, consider my current food philosophy.

Nettye's Faithfully Fit Food Philosophy

1. Eat foods as close to the way God put them here.
2. Embrace moderation.
3. Eat mindfully and thankfully.

Experience and observations have solidified the first two points as constants in my philosophy. The third changes as needed to address current needs, goals, or challenges.

I believe clean eating and moderation are game changers in weight management. Let's unpack these concepts.

Eat foods as close to the way God put them here

While raised in Chicago, I have country roots. Our backyard was *Green Eighth-of-an-Acre*. Our landscaping was edible. Even as a young child, I found something glorious in the ability to walk by a cherry tomato plant in our yard and pluck off a few ripe pieces of fruit, to rub them on my pants and throw them in my mouth. The pop and explosion of sweetness and acidity was a beautiful thing. The tomato experience in ketchup squirted on a burger or atop a mound of fries just isn't the same.

God is so good to us. He lovingly provides us with an abundance of foods with glorious textures, flavor profiles, and sensory and aesthetic properties.

What God made is good.

> [11]Then God said, "Let the land produce vegetation: seed-bearing plants and trees on the land that bear fruit with seed in it, according to their various kinds." And it was so. [12]The land produced vegetation: plants bearing seed according to their kinds and trees bearing fruit with seed in it according to their kinds. And God saw that it was good. Genesis 1:11-12

Harm happens when we distance ourselves from God's provisions.

Harm happens when we distance ourselves from God's provisions. As this relates to food, in general, the further we get from the whole or natural food (the food God created), the less healthful the food becomes.

Nutritional science affirms this truth over and over, and the whole food or clean eating movement encapsulates this reality. Some point to nature as the source. In truth, the goodness is ascribed to God, who created and sustains nature.

By and large, we have left the real food table provided by our Father and ventured into the far country to dine at the food industry's table of fake food. The *American Journal of Clinical Nutrition* reports that 61 percent of the calories eaten come solely from highly processed food.

Food scientist and former chief technical officer for Pillsbury James Behnke calls the "big tenets" of the food industry 'taste, convenience and cost." Not nutrition. Foods from cereals, to soft drinks; heat-and-eat entrees to boxed macaroni and cheese; frozen seasoned vegetables to jarred pasta sauce—these foods prepared for us have been engineered to hook us. They have been jacked up with scientifically determined amounts of salt, sugar, and fat to drive cravings and overindulgence. Food engineers call it the "bliss point."

In Michael Moss' book *Salt, Sugar, Fat,* Harvard's Department of Nutrition chair, Walter Willet, points the finger of blame for the nation's rise in obesity and related decline in health at the food companies. "The transition of food to being an industrial product really has been a fundamental problem," Willett said. "First, the actual processing has stripped away the nutritional value of the food. Most of the grains have been converted to starches. We have sugar in concentrated form, and most of the fats have been concentrated and then, worst of all, hydrogenated, which creates trans-fatty acids with very adverse effects on health."[52]

This is evil. And we walk into it unaware.

But we can't just point the finger at the corporate food industry. Manufacturers make the substandard food. We buy it. We eat it. We feed it to our children.

We also replicate the stripping of nutrition from food in our kitchens.

Consider a fresh, ripe, in-season peach. What a wonderful creation—a conglomeration of textures and tastes from the fuzzy tart skin to the silky sweet flesh. When you bite into it and the juice runs down your hand, it's just glorious.

Most often, we don't buy a fresh peach. We get canned peaches, jacked up with sugar in that heavy syrup. But let's suppose this time, we have fresh peaches. How often would they be sliced and enjoyed as a dessert in their natural form? It is far more probable that the peach will get peeled (fiber), covered in refined sugar and butter (saturated fat), and baked in a crust of refined white flour and more butter. When it is done, we'll top it off with a scoop of ice cream. The nutrition of the overall dish is pitiful and the flavor of the peach is overshadowed by sugar, fat, and salt—which drives our cravings.

Highly nutritious cruciferous broccoli gets cooked limp and smothered in fatty, salty cheese sauce or ranch dressing. Overcooking diminishes nutritional value. And the sauce reduces the nutrient and caloric density and dulls our tastes away from the God-given flavor of broccoli. Instead, we taste the salt and fat components and crave the salt and fat more.

One more example. Consider bacon. You can't cut a pig and chow down. For safety, the flesh has to be butchered, cured, and cooked. Even then, as bacon cooks, God made it such that the heart-hurting saturated fat melts and falls away from the flesh. Yet we collect it, store it, and pour it into healthy vegetables—and call it seasoning.

We unknowingly and consistently take steps far, far away from food's God-given tastes and nutrition. Our weight, health, and well-being suffer.

Eating foods close to the way God put them here reverses this harm. Choose a peach more often than peach cobbler a la mode. Eat crisp steamed or roasted broccoli with lemon instead of limp cheese sauce-drowned broccoli. Choose herbs to season dishes instead of old pork-saturated fat.

To get the body God intends for us, we must take steps back to provisions He has made for that body.

This works for my weight management and health, so this is the first rule in my food philosophy. Does it seem like an effective fit for yours?

Embrace Moderation

After the birth of our baby girl, my life was out of control. Work was increasingly demanding, requiring up to 70 percent out-of-state travel. Giving time and attention to my husband and two small children, service at church, work life, personal development, and self-care was kicking my butt. Guess what was the first thing to fall off the list? *Ding, ding ding!* Personal care. My body was a wreck and my sanity was not far behind. I'll spare the gory details, but I could not keep it all together. I could not find balance.

As the Holy Spirit spoke repeatedly to my hard-to-hear, slow-to-listen, resistant-to-respond self, a song by Ted Winn became my balm. I'd play it while driving to meetings with tears rolling down my face. I'd listen to it to pump me up when I'd wake up tired with a full day of tasks ahead. I'd go over the words in my head to calm frazzled nerves when I was about go off on somebody (*okay—after I went off on someone*). The song was on repeat. Here are some of the lyrics.

> *For every summer day, there's a winter night.*
> *Somedays everything goes wrong, somedays everything goes right.*
> *For every mountain high, there's a valley low.*
> *Remember that you will reap what you sow.*
> *So every weekday life is filled give and take*
> *And it's a game of balance that we all must play.*
> *Live your life with balance. (6x)*
> *Everybody oughta live, live a balanced life.*
>
> *Spend some time with friends and time with family.*
> *Don't forget that alone time we all need.*
> *Learn from your experience pass the wisdom on.*
> *Everybody's father has been somebody's son.*
> *Take some time to reflect, time to reminisce.*
> *Appreciate the present, the future is a gift.*
> *Live your life with balance. (6x)*
> *Everybody oughta live, live a balanced life.*
>
> *Have respect for nature, this world is not your own.*
> *We all share this planet so treat it like your own.*
>
> *There is a lesson that I hope you will learn.*
> *From the heart of this song every note every word.*
> *That you live your life with no apology,*
> *And strike a balance that is perfect harmony.*[53]

The song closes with a vamp of a dozen repeats of the encouragement to "live your life with balance" followed by repeated affirmations that "I will live my life with balance." (Did you catch the name of the song is "Balance"?)

Balance. Moderation. What is life without it?

Somewhere, somehow, we get it in our minds that we are supposed to be on 10 all the time. Constantly going. Constantly doing. Constantly on focus. Constantly on point. Departures from full throttle are signs of weakness or indicators of failure.

Lies!

God doesn't intend for His creation to be on all the time. He gave us the example of work and rest with the seventh day, with His creation of *menuha*, Sabbath rest, tranquility, serenity, peace, and repose.[54]

God created nature to flow with seasons. Times of growth and development, times of production. Times of degeneration and regeneration.

Scripture records periods of service and of celebration. Famines as well as feasts. The wisdom recorded in Ecclesiastes says it well.

> [1]*There is a time for everything,*
>   *and a season for every activity under the heavens:*
> [2] *a time to be born and a time to die,*
>   *a time to plant and a time to uproot,*
> [3] *a time to kill and a time to heal,*
>   *a time to tear down and a time to build,*
> [4] *a time to weep and a time to laugh,*
>   *a time to mourn and a time to dance,*
> [11] *He has made everything beautiful in its time. He has also set eternity in the human heart; yet no one can fathom what God has done from beginning to end.* [12] *I know that there is nothing better for people than to be happy and to do good while they live.* [13] *That each of them may eat and drink, and find satisfaction in all their toil— this is the gift of God.*
> Ecclesiastes 3:1-4, 11-13

Everything is beautiful in its time. That's moderation.

Perhaps you've seen people who run themselves into the ground— folks who refuse to sit down, so they get laid down. It takes illness for them to rest and listen. Maybe you've been that person. I've been there.

All or nothing sounds fierce. It may make you feel strong and productive. But all or nothing typical goes from all to nothing.

Relate this to food. You have a plan. You are motivated, focused, and doing this thing. Give it time.

Without moderation, motivation about that eating pattern changes to frustration with that eating pattern. Hence the start and stop and start over, again. Up and down goes your weight. Bring out the yo-yo.

God created food for our nutrition *and enjoyment.* Moderation makes space for those celebrations and feasts. It provides margin in which motivation can be renewed. Moderation makes healthy and productive lifestyles maintainable and enjoyable.

If you enjoy that peach cobbler with ice cream, have some. Periodically. That's moderation and balance.

Moderation means different things to different people. For each individual, moderation can be dynamic, changing with the season and circumstances of life.

Finding your place of moderation

First and foremost, pray and listen for the Holy Spirit's guidance. He will lead you to that place of repose.

Consider the Pareto principle. Also called the 80/20 rule, the Pareto principle is a typical distribution found to be effective in many areas. For example, it is said that:

- Eighty percent of a country's wealth is controlled by 20 percent of the population.
- Eighty percent of sales come from 20 percent of a company's customer base.
- Eighty percent of complaints received come from 20 percent of the customers.
- Some suggest in many churches that 20 percent of the membership does 80 percent of the service in ministry.

This ratio is an effective way to bring moderation to weight loss and weight management. You may choose to make healthful food choices 80 percent of the time and reserve 20 percent of eating for more indulgent selections. You may opt daily to eat clean for breakfast, lunch, and dinner and have one processed snack or dessert. Focused weekday and fun weekend eating is another version of the 80/20 rule. A few weeks ago, when my dairy consumption (cheese) got my body to balking, I removed dairy two days per week (and included cheese if I wanted it the other five days). That 80/20 split struck a balance between what I wanted and what my body tolerated.

A caution on that 20 percent: Indulgences or splurges are just that. They are not open invitations for gluttony. Eighty percent wise eating will not make up for 20 percent buck wild eating. Moreover, gluttony is spiritual as well as physical. Don't give place or a foothold to that sin.

A third help key to moderation is consistent feedback. Information on how the changes in behavior affect overall progress is critical.

In surveying people who successfully maintain significant weight loss, the National Weight Control Registry found that 75 percent report that they weigh themselves regularly, at least once per week. Changes outside normal weight fluctuation can be addressed with simple adjustments. Another relatively common pattern for people who struggle with weight is to not weigh for long periods. When they get on the scale, they are shocked. It is easier to address five pounds than it is to address 15 or 25.

Eat mindfully and thankfully

As mentioned, the third element of my philosophy changes to fit what is going on. The time, mental challenges, and stress that came with the writing of this book took me out of my normal. When tired or stuck on a certain passage, before I'd know it, I'd walk into the kitchen and get a snack. For me, this is a slippery slope. Even though the choices were healthy, eating when I'm not hungry is an old habit I don't want back.

So I set focus on mindfulness and thankfulness as a shield against that which I know whips my tail. This means taking pause before I chew to notice I am about to eat (sounds ridiculous, right?). It means not just saying grace before I chow down, but to pause and truly give thanks. This pause stops autopilot and acknowledges God in the situation. In the moment, I forget the issue at hand is not hunger, it is fatigue, stress, or frustration while writing. The refreshing I need is not in the pantry.

Your turn.

Your food philosophy is your weapon to put down weight loss and health-hindering behaviors. To get to it, start by seeing your patterns and identifying what helps and harms your progress. Choose a few (two to four) elements that will take you to success.

A few tips.

- If you don't know what to include, that's okay. Pray about it, and as you continue through the information and self-examination exercises in this book, take note of recurring patterns in your responses and actions the Holy Spirit lays on your heart. In the interim, feel free to use the first two elements outlined in this chapter. Adopt them as a start. Keep it manageable.

- As you begin to draft your philosophy, be sure to state values in the positive. Don't focus on what you are not going to do. State what you will focus on, the value you will uphold. For example: If you are led to address your emotional eating, instead of statements like *Stop Emotional Eating* or *Don't Respond to Emotions with Food*, you might opt for *Appropriately Feed the Need.*

- Be somewhat specific. The philosophy is not a list of action steps; it is a set of values that will guide actions. That said, the value statements can't be so vague that action is lost. Statements like *Eat healthy* or *Honor God* are great values, but standing alone, they are too far reaching. Dig in for more clarity on those statements.

- Make it God focused. Apart from Him we can do nothing.

My Faithfully Fit Food Philosophy

1. _____

_____

_____

2. _____

_____

_____

3. _____

_____

_____

Praction (Prayer - Action)

Journal your thoughts, prayer, and plan of action from this section.

CHAPTER 7

Define Your Food Groove

"To change your life, change your habits."
Unknown

STUDIES INDICATE THAT THIN people are creatures of habit.

Cognitive behavior expert and author of *The Beck Diet Solution: Train Your Brain to Think Like a Thin Person* Judith Beck, PhD, explains, "Thin people have what I call a food groove—the majority of their meals consist of well-planned staples."[55] Variances and indulgences are sprinkled in here and there, but by and large, daily eating is built around a core group of meals and snacks that support their healthy body.

I adopted this habit years ago, and it benefits my hips and head. Most days I cycle through three to five favorite breakfasts, lunches, dinners, and snacks that taste good and are healthy, enjoyable, and a good fit for my budget and lifestyle. One or two times a week, I indulge my burgeoning fit foodie and deliberately go way off the grid, trying an ingredient I've never had or creating new recipes. This balance allows me to explore food and keeps my weight stable. But here's the big bonus: I don't waste time or energy planning, thinking, or worrying about what I am going to eat. It helps keep food in its place, and I recommend this habit to my clients.

Do you think about food—a lot? This may help you. Here are two methods to develop a food groove.

Food Type Method

My food groove is built upon types of foods based upon my tastes and what is in season at the time. For example, in the summer, lunch may involve some kind of a smoothie, salad, wrap, or stir-fry. In the few cool months we get in Louisiana, lunch leans more towards soups, sandwiches, grains, or root vegetable-based salads or casseroles. With a healthfully stocked kitchen and type of food in mind, I can open the fridge or pantry and pull together a great meal without much time or thought. This method is a good fit for those who want a bit of versatility in their food habit.

Give it a try.

Step 1: In the chart, define five to seven meal ideas or snacks that:

- You enjoy (you won't eat what you don't like).
- You eat regularly (in line with your preferences).
- Are readily available (include a pack 'n' go or restaurant option if this is needed for your lifestyle).

Breakfasts	Lunches	Dinners	Snacks

Step 2: Edit your selections.

- Remove items that are not in line with your Faithfully Fit Food Philosophy (see chapter 6). For example, if one of your goals is to limit refined sugar, but donuts appear in your breakfast column because a donut and coffee is your breakfast a few days a week at work, cross it off. This does not mean you will never eat donuts—but they should not be a regular in your eating. That donut can be an occasional indulgence.

- Make swaps or add items that bring health and balance to your daily eating. Example: if one of your go-to lunches is a burger and fries, consider swapping a side salad or fruit for the fries.

- Try to include vegetables and/or fruit at each meal.

- Continue to edit until you have three to five healthy options you will eat and enjoy.

- Remember, this is your regular list. It should reflect good stewardship. Make sure it includes foods that progress your goals and nurture the temple of the Holy Spirit.

Step 3: Update the list as the change of seasons, food availability, your tastes, and lifestyle dictate.

To give you a sample, check out what I'm eating this week. Note: my schedule is crazy busy as I'm deep into writing, so I automatically limited options to a few fast and satisfying selections.

Breakfasts:

- Smoothie – a quick easy way to get fruits, veggies, and energy for the day. A couple of my favorite smoothies follow this chapter.

- Everything muffin – I make and freeze a big batch of these every few weeks. Recipe also provided after this chapter.

- Toasted sandwich and apple – current sandwich favorites, egg sandwich, or a peanut butter and honey sandwich, or avocado spread on rye toast. Gala and Honeycrisp apples are in season and on sale right now.

Lunches

- Salads – Greek salad, or leftover side dish over mixed greens. (Example – yesterday I enjoyed quinoa tabbouleh leftover from Sunday's dinner on top of a mix of kale and spinach.)
- Soup – From the freezer, homemade potato broccoli, carrot ginger, or tomato vegetable white bean soup. (*Each time I make soup, I cook a double batch and freeze individual servings for busy times like these.*) In the pantry – several cans of Amy's Kitchen soup and a few cartons of Trader Joe's soups. (*Both brands are delicious.*)
- Veggie burger and fruit. I keep Morningstar Farms or Trader Joe's veggie burgers in the freezer or swing by Mooyah Burger for a fast food option.

Dinners

I'm nursing a huge pot of greens (mustard and collards) and cornbread alongside:

- Lentil shepherd's pie (made three weeks ago and frozen).
- Beans and brown rice.
- Sautéed vegetables with brown rice and hummus.

Snacks

- Dried fruit and mixed nuts.
- Vegetable crudité and pita with hummus.
- Homemade granola.
- Everything muffins.

Initially, the list-making will be a planned, deliberate process. Habits become automatic with repetition. In time, the choices will be concrete, and your healthy eating routine will fall into place.

Weekly Meal Prep Method

Weekly meal prep is another way to develop a food groove. Here you plan, prepare, and pack away the meals you will eat later in the week. This method is a big time saver, as daily meals are grab-and-go or heat-and-eat.

This method has recently soared in popularity. Google "meal prep" or do a search for it on Pinterest. The volume and variety of results will blow your mind and make your mouth water. This is a fantastic option for people with busy schedules and those who thrive on structure or predictability.

Helpful meal prep tools:

- **Mason jars.** Meal preppers use these for make-ahead salads. Put the salad dressing in the bottom. Next, add sturdy vegetables or grains (for example, broccoli, cucumbers, beans, rice, quinoa). Continue layering with other salad ingredients, with the most delicate and wiltable items on top (for example, the salad greens). Screw on the lid and store in the fridge. The jars look so pretty, and here's the good part: when ready to eat, just shake the jar. Every part of the salad will be beautifully dressed.

- **Bowls with lids** are perfect for hearty and healthy burrito bowl or rice bowl dishes.

- **Divided storage containers** prevent the meal components from getting tossed together.

- Use **muffin tin liners** to bake individual omelets or frittatas as well as muffins or quick breads.

- A **planning calendar and shopping list** helps the process run smoothly. Post a magnetic whiteboard with the days of the week on your refrigerator. At the top of the board, post a scripture or quote that sets the tone of your stewardship for that week. Plan and record the meals under each day. At the bottom, collect your shopping list of ingredients and items needed to make the meals happen. Snap a picture of the board for the shopping trip to the grocer and farmer's market. Shop, wash, chop, cook, pack, and store your meals. You are good to go. The posted plan on the fridge eliminates guesswork and takes a load off your memory. Each time you walk in the kitchen, healthy options greet you at the fridge. Keeping your goal or plan in front of you can also help shut down temptations.

Making it work

These are just two of the many paths to a food habit.

My household requires a hybrid approach. I'm vegetarian. My husband and children are not, so at times I prepare different items for my meals. Additionally, I'm comfortable with leftovers and meal repeats. Our children—not so much. Here is how I make it work.

Each week, we plan the family meals as a family. I make it a point to involve my husband (so he gets what he wants) and the children (to take advantage of the teachable moments created around food). During this planning, we discuss the inclusion of healthy foods at all meals along with periodic treats for balance, and I expand the children's palates and try to get them excited about trying new foods. The family food plan is written down and used to guide weekend grocery shopping and daily cooking for the week.

My food "plan" lives primarily in my head and is not as structured. Repeating food types has become habit. I automatically cycle through a few meals based upon my schedule, tastes, a new recipe idea I want to try, or what is growing in my garden or fresh at the farmer's market.

The key is to set the intent, then find a way that works for you.

Examine Thyself

Do you believe the food type or meal prep method would be helpful to you? Why or why not?

If yes, list three benefits you would gain from developing a food groove.

1. _____

2. _____

3. _____

What may hinder this process?

How can you work around the obstacle(s)?

Praction (Prayer - Action)

Journal your thoughts, prayer, and plan of action from this section.

Recipe: Everything Muffins

These vegan muffins are chock full of fruit, vegetables, fiber, and flavor—with no refined sugar. Great for breakfast, dessert, or a snack, they are moist, sweet, nutty, and super-satisfying. These muffins are everything!
(Makes 12-15 muffins.)

Ingredients:

2 tablespoons canola or coconut oil
1 super-ripe banana, mashed
¼ cup unsweetened applesauce
¼ cup date paste (see notes)
2 teaspoons pure vanilla extract
1 cup grated zucchini
1 cup grated Honeycrisp apple

1 ½ cups unbleached flour
½ teaspoon baking soda
½ teaspoon salt
2 teaspoons ground cinnamon
¼ cup golden raisins
¼ cup apple juice-infused dried cranberries (see notes)
½ cup toasted walnuts, chopped

Instructions:

Preheat oven to 350 degrees.

In large bowl, stir oil, mashed banana, applesauce, and date paste until combined. Fold in grated zucchini and apple. Set aside.

In another bowl, sift dry ingredients - flour, salt, baking soda, and cinnamon. Add dry ingredients to wet ingredients. Stir carefully to combine, being careful not to overmix. Mixture will be stiff. If too thick, add a tablespoon of water at a time (up to three) to loosen it up a bit.

Stir in nuts, raisins, and cranberries. Spoon ¼ cup measures into muffin tin. (If tin is metal, use muffin liners or lightly oil tin before adding batter.)

Bake 15-20 minutes or until a toothpick inserted in muffin comes out almost clean. Cool and remove from tin. The fruit/zucchini content and absence of egg make these muffins super-moist and dense.

Date paste is a delicious and versatile natural sweetener. To make date paste, place 5-6 Medjool dates in a small saucepan. Add ½ cup water. Lightly simmer for 10 minutes until soft. Allow to cool. Remove pits and place dates in food processor. Drizzle in reserved cooking water and pulse until smooth mixture is formed. Five to six Medjool dates yield 1/3 cup date paste. Date paste can be stored in refrigerator for up to 1 week.

Dried cranberries. Due to the tart flavor of cranberries, dried cranberries are sweetened - typically with refined sugar. I prefer dried cranberries sweetened with apple juice.

Toasting nuts intensifies the flavor. Place nuts in dry skillet over medium heat. Slowly toast for a minute or two stirring frequently to prevent burning. Your nose will tell you when they are ready. Be careful not to burn the nuts. Doing so turns them horribly bitter.

Recipe: Super, Simple Smoothies

A smoothie is basically a thick drink made by pulverizing fruit, vegetables, seeds and/or nuts with a liquid and something frozen in a strong blender until smooth. I adore smoothies because they:

Taste like a milkshake or fruity slushy drink.

Are fast and easy to make.

Can be nutritious and filling.

Allow you to sip your servings of fruits or vegetables and,

Did I mention they taste like a milkshake or fruity slushy drink?

Variations are limitless and the drink can be as healthy or indulgent as you like based on the selected ingredients. I have several smoothie cookbooks and sometimes hook up something exotic (*The Blender Girl* by Tess Masters is wonderful). Most of the time, my smoothies are simple. I like dairy-free, refined sugar-free, vegan smoothies that taste indulgent. Here are a few of my favorite combinations.

First start with a base.

Simple Smoothie Base

(Serves one)

1 frozen banana

1-2 dates (I like Medjool dates. Remove the pit and soak them first for a smoother blend.)

1 cup ice

1 - 1 ½ cup unsweetened almond milk

½ - 1 scoop plant-based protein powder (optional)

Use this simple smoothie base as a foundation and play. Example variations:

Smoothie	Variation Ingredients
Vanilla Smoothie	Splash of vanilla extract Light grating of fresh nutmeg (optional)
Chocolate Nut Butter Smoothie	1 Tbsp. cocoa powder 1 Tbsp. natural peanut or almond butter
Green Goodness Smoothie	1 cup spinach ¼ ripe avocado
Berry Baby Smoothie	1 cup frozen berry mix No-sugar-added apple juice (as needed)
Pumpkin Spice Smoothie	¼ cup canned pumpkin A sprinkle of pumpkin pie spice Grade B maple syrup (as needed)

VALUE
THE BLESSING
OF FOOD

CHAPTER 8

Experience Food

Food: "God's love made edible."
Norman Wirzba

AT MY LAST CORPORATE position, the executive managers loved wine and held several manager–teambuilding events at wineries. I don't drink and throw no shade to those who do in moderation. Drinking wine is not a sin—getting drunk is. (Ephesians 5:18, Proverbs 20:1, 1 Timothy 5:23, John 2:1-11). Passing on alcohol is a personal decision made because I tried it, don't like it (physically, socially, or spiritually), and I prefer to chew and get nutrition from my calories.

Back to the winery.

For a non-drinker, one would think these events would be a drag. To the contrary, I found the wine tastings fascinating. The sommelier's stories were informative—explaining how different varieties of their wine were made, detailing the flavor notes, and painting a picture with words about the experience in the glass. Watching the tasters was more interesting. They would swirl the wine to increase and release aroma compounds into the air. Next, they'd take careful note of the color, clarity, and viscosity of the wine, examining the density of legs formed in the glass. Finally, they would take a sniff, noting the aroma followed by a series of sips and slurps (and what looked to me like a dainty mouthwash gargle) to aerate the wine, put it on different parts of the tongue to isolate the notes, tones, and aftertaste. For the wine connoisseur, details matter—from the type of wood the wine barrel is made from to the shape of the glass it is served in. It was an involved process that the participants truly enjoyed. Their appreciation for the wine and the winemakers was evident. And in all the wine tastings I attended, no one overindulged and got lit.

Contrast this with the wino experience.

I grew up on the Southside of Chicago and on regular walks to public transportation along 79th Street, I'd pass several establishments that sold alcohol. Periodically, outside would sit a patron or two, pushed up against the wall of the building or in the shade of a tree in a nearby vacant lot—"tasting" their purchase. These wine experiences looked quite different. No swirls, slow sips, and slurps. Gulps and guzzles were the form. From the empty bottles that littered the area, it didn't appear the drinkers preferred a particular variety or producer. Type of glass wasn't a consideration—drinking from the bottle wrapped in a brown bag was just fine. Cheap and abundant seemed most important.

In explaining what I saw on the street outside the liquor stores, please know it is not my intent to make light of this heavy situation. As a child, this scene was a part of the landscape of our neighborhood. I can't say it was the norm, but it wasn't uncommon. Their demeanor was usually jovial, throwing nonsensical and sometimes humorous words at passersby. I didn't see danger or feel threatened. Sadly, I also did not feel the desperation or recognize the bondage before me. I didn't see a person caught up and trapped by a need to feed the call of the flesh.

When it comes to food, are your actions more in line with the wine connoisseur or the wino?

What are you looking for when you eat: quality, value, and an enjoyable experience or junk in abundance?

Do you take the time to savor and enjoy the experience? Are you mindful of the food and consciously grateful to the Creator of the food (and I don't mean the cook), or are your meals and snacks too often rapidly gobbled from a paper bag without thought or thanks?

The wine connoisseur values and controls the experience.

Value is lost to the wino, who is controlled by the substance.

With food, I've been like that wino. I've been like that wino. I have been that wino!!! Many times, I've been at my desk with a bag of something, deeply focused on a task, and before I know it, I have greasy fingers, an empty bag, and my mind is wondering, "Where in the world did it go?" Or the items eaten while driving. Or the meals eaten so fast that shortly afterwards I am mentally hungry and go looking for something else. Anyone with me here?

We can't put food on "Team Too Much"—giving it too much power, too much focus, and too much control in our lives. The flipside is just as harmful to weight maintenance. We must be careful not to take this aspect of our everyday living (we have to eat to stay alive) and dilute it to the point that it becomes mindless. *Example/sharing/confession: Three weeks ago, tired from a week of long days at a conference, I drove the nine-hour trek from Nashville, Tennessee, to Baton Rouge, Louisiana. Behind that steering wheel, I turned into a neat version of the cookie monster with a small bag of nostalgic candy from Cracker Barrel.*

If you can relate, come with me off the street into the vineyard to experience food.

Mindful Eating

Mindful eating is a vital weight management principle. When we engage the mind as well as the mouth and belly, smaller amounts of food satisfy. Some experts believe mindful eating brings a balance and takes and keeps excess pounds off.

The chefs on the Food Network have helped me greatly in this area. Yep. As they present food, they describe the item and break down the flavor profiles, detailing how it affects their palette. They define qualities that work well together or don't. *Another example/sharing/confession: When cooking and eating, I often pretend I'm on the Food Network. I do this so often that our children probably think the commentary is part of the cooking process. In my head, I'm a mix of the calm elegance of Ina Garten with the wit of Damaris Phillips. In reality, I'm neither.* Nonetheless, as I cook and eat, *I* break the food down in my mind and verbalize what is being experienced. Sensory analysis of food slows eating, adds to the enjoyment, and increases cooking skill.

To eat mindfully, notice the look, smell, texture, and taste of what you consume.

Look

When you eat at an excellent restaurant, recall the care chefs take to make the meals attractive. It adds to the experience. Hook your plates up at home. Make your food pretty.

Include multiple colors in your meals. It adds nutrition as well as visual appeal.

Plate your food. Don't eat from a bag or box. Put the food on an attractive plate. White plates make the food pop, but studies show people who eat from brightly colored plates eat less (red plates cause the least amount of overeating). Size also matters. Dinner plates are huge, so reasonable portions look minuscule. Use a smaller salad plate to trick the eye. Less food looks like more.

Artfully prep the food. I'm not suggesting you carve edible rose buds for garnish. Just take a moment to make the food look interesting.

Aroma

Taste and smell work together when we eat. Notice how you can barely taste food when you have a stuffy nose. The olfactory tract, an area of nerve cells at the top of the nasal cavities, detects thousands of chemical compounds and routes them to the brain with information from the taste buds. Together olfactory stimuli (smell), gustatory stimuli (taste), and temperature stimuli combine to create flavor. Before you take the first bite of food, take in a whiff. Give time and opportunity for both senses to engage.

Texture

What textures do you prefer? Crunchy, crisp, chewy, creamy? Do you prefer a single texture on your plate or a variety? Notice how the feel of food in your mouth adds to the experience.

Taste

Humans experience five basic types of tastes: saltiness (from sodium, chlorine, potassium, and magnesium), sweet (from sugar derivatives as well as some amino acids and proteins), sour (from the hydrogen ions in acidic items), bitter (from over 30 proteins), and umami (a savory taste from glutamic acid or aspartic acid).

Taste buds on our tongue have sensory cells that respond to the five tastes at ten levels of intensity. This yields 100,000 combinations.[56] *Isn't that amazing!*

Food is a gift from God. Scripture records food as the first gift of creation. As John Bishop writes, "Open a Bible to Genesis 1 and look at what God does in the creation story. More specifically, look at the verbs: God creates, he hovers, he says, he names, he separates, he makes and blesses and sees and declares it good. But it isn't until the end of the chapter, in verse 29, that he gives. And what does he give? Food."[57]

> *Then God said, "I give you every seed-bearing plant on the face of the whole earth and every tree that has fruit with seed in it. They will be yours for food.* Genesis 1:29

Norman Wirzba, the author of *Food and Faith: A Theology of Eating*, calls food "God's love made edible." He blessed us with a bounty of foods and huge variances of flavors, not just for nutritional needs. It is also given for our enjoyment.

Experience and enjoy this beautiful gift.

Examine Thyself

Are there times you feel out of control with food? If so, record instances that trigger this situation.

Do you eat mindlessly? If so, what times or circumstances support this behavior?

With the conscious realization that food is a gift from God, what steps will you take to enjoy the blessing and be mindful and thankful for food?

1. _____

2. _____

3. _____

Praction (Prayer - Action)

Journal your thoughts, prayer, and plan of action from this section.

Recipe Remake - Black Bean Soup

Very high in fiber, folate, protein, and antioxidants, black beans are good for you and just plain good in this easy soup. The recipe is a knock-off of the black bean soup served at Lone Star Steakhouse. It takes just a few ingredients but is full of flavor and fiber. One of my favorites.

Makes approximately one large or two small servings

Ingredients:

For the soup:
1 (15-ounce) can black beans
¼ red onion, chopped (divided, set aside about 1 teaspoon of the chopped onion for garnish)
1 clove garlic, minced
½ teaspoon red wine vinegar
¼ teaspoon sugar
¼ teaspoon chili powder
Pinch of cayenne pepper (about ⅛ tsp)
Chopped pickled peppers (divided, set aside about 1 teaspoon of the chopped peppers for garnish)
> *Note: Most of the time, I use jarred jalapeño slices (the kind used on nachos). Jarred mild banana pepper rings and jarred Golden Greek Pepperoncini Tempero peppers are excellent as well.*

For the garnish:
Reserved chopped red onion (about 1 tsp)
Reserved chopped peppers (about 1 tsp)
Small dollop of light sour cream (about ½ tsp)
Bit of chopped cilantro

Instructions:
> Add the can of black beans (including the juice), and all the other soup ingredients in a saucepan.

> Stir and bring to a boil.

> Turn the heat down to low and simmer uncovered for about 45 minutes to let the flavors meld and develop.

> Stir periodically and add a bit of water if it gets too thick.

That's it. Put it in a bowl, add your garnish, and enjoy. The soup is fantastic with a piece of cornbread or tortilla chips.

CHAPTER 9

Explore Food

"I did then what I knew how to do.
Now that I know better, I do better."
Maya Angelou

HAVE YOU EVER HEARD the story of Big Mama and the Christmas ham? Here is a version modified from *A Tale of the Tail, Daughters and Mothers: Taking the Next Step*:

> The family was poor, but Big Mama was a master at making little seem like much. Christmas was ultra-special for the family and every year she took pride in laying out a full table centered around a big Christmas ham. As Big Mama cooked, the three girls in the family learned and helped. In preparing the ham for the oven, Big Mama would ceremoniously sharpen her big knife, cut the ends off the ham, and place the ham in the pan. It always turned out perfect and Christmas dinner was full of good food, laughs, and love.

> The three daughters grew up, excelled in school, and had busy lives and careers. They held on to the cherished tradition of Big Mama's Christmas dinner and passed it along to their daughters. The year after Big Mama's passing, the family decided to get together for Christmas. It was tough finding a real ham, but they did, and the granddaughters argued over who would get to prepare it.

> Watching the good-natured fight over the big knife, Melvin (newly married into the family) asked why everyone wanted the knife. "To cut the ends off the ham," someone replied.

Melvin asked, "Why do you cut the ends off the ham?"

"It allows steam to get out," one granddaughter replied.

"No, girl! It lets the heat in so it cooks through," another said.

Realizing they were making the reasons up, they asked their mothers. "Why do we cut the ends off the ham?"

"Because Big Mama always did—that's what made it taste so good," was the reply.

Wanting a definitive answer, the granddaughters went to their grandfather, who was rocking in a chair by the fire and asked, "Paw-Paw, do you know why Big Mama cut the ends off the ham?"

"Of course," he replied. "Because her pan was too small."

Exploring the Tradition of Food

I imagine everyone can relate to this story in some area of life.
We do x because we have always done x.
We don't question x.
We make up reasons validating x, and pass the practice of x to others.
I've experienced this with food.

My parents were born in the '20s and '30s in Amite County, Mississippi. I was bred on down-home, old-fashioned Southern values ... and cooking. I thank God for my upbringing. The standards, experiences, and memories laid a fantastic foundation that my husband and I gratefully share with our children.

While I enjoy the tastes, textures, and memories of good soul food, the strong pattern of hypertension and diabetes in my family health tree, as well as the overweight and heart condition in my life, called for a closer look at the food I had given a hallowed place. It was easy to see that a diet full of things fried, smothered, candied, or porked was good *to* me, but not good *for* me.

Does "good to you but not so good for you" apply to some foods of your tradition?

Food, culture, tradition, and history unite on our plates, and the passage of recipes connects generations. There is value in history and things of old—but we truly honor and benefit when we look at the *roots* of tradition and examine if and how it is best applied in our lives today.

For example, in my culture, African-Americans trace our food history to the period of enslavement, when our ancestors survived on scraps, leftovers, and undesirable, unhealthy cuts of meat. Lard (included in rations) and gravied stews (used to stretch meats) were common in preparations. Chitterlings (that is, hog intestines), pig feet, and pigtails were seasoned and turned into delicacies. These and many other vestiges of bondage remain in our culinary experiences today. Many value and enjoy these foods and preparations and call it our culture. Scrap foods and health-harming foods are celebrated as our history. It is not working well for us. We fail to recognize that our genetic history predates slavery. Chef and educator Bryant Terry argues that the disconnect from historical foods of the African diaspora is a contributing factor to the increase of chronic illnesses affecting African-American communities.[58]

In all cultures, the celebration of traditional cuisine should be informed and holistic. Incorporating culturally appropriate foods can add to health and weight loss instead of harm it. Like the women in the story who cut the end of the ham because they had to, some of the foods and preparations many cultures hold so dear came from "had to" situations. God has blessed beyond "had to." Our actions should reflect thankfulness and good stewardship.

Don't get me wrong—if one so chooses, a hog maw in the pot every once in a while adds balance and flavor to eating. But practices we know are not good for us should not be regular.

When we know better, we must choose better.

Shift your food focus from blindly following tradition to mindfully exploring the tradition of your cultural cooking.

Shift from blindly following tradition to mindfully exploring tradition.

God has blessed us with an abundance of foods. I thoroughly enjoy trying new foods and exploring new preparations for soul food standards. My family continues to enjoy traditional foods, but not every day. Those meals are reserved for holidays, and many of the recipes have been adjusted for better nutrition. (I make a mean lean gumbo!)

Do some of the traditional foods you enjoy add to your weight and/or decrease your health?

List the most frequently eaten "good to you but not so good for you" traditional foods in the box below. We will revisit the list at the end of this chapter.

Exploring Food

Traditional foods are not the only culprit. Foods relatively new on the scene also do a number on our bodies. USDA Economic Research Service data indicates that 63 percent of the American diet is comprised of processed foods. Many of these foods are packed with chemicals, additives, and preservatives to change textures or flavor, retain freshness, and extend the shelf life. The Food and Drug

Administration requires the labeling of ingredients and nutrient levels on most processed foods.

Important information about the packaged foods we put in our body is right there on the label. Do you read it? Do you know what is in your food?

Our people perish for lack of knowledge.

Don't get hoodwinked by claims on the front of the package and assume buzzword claims mean the food supports health or weight loss.

- "Sugar free" items are typically hyped up on fat.

- "Fat free" items are usually loaded with sugar.

- The label "all natural" is largely open to interpretation. For example, some companies consider high-fructose corn syrup as natural because it is made from corn.

- If overall sugar is a concern in your diet, "No sugar added" labeling may not help. This means refined sugar was not added. Milk sugar (lactose) or sugar from fruit (fructose) may still be present.

- "Zero trans fat" means the food contains less than 0.5 grams per serving. If the package contains more than two servings, the food provides an unsafe amount of trans fat.

- "Light" means the fat content is 50 percent less than the amount in comparable products. This could still be a significant amount of fat.

- "Lightly sweetened" is not defined by the Food and Drug Administration, so basically it means whatever the manufacturer wants it to mean.

Terms on the front of the package are largely marketing-driven terms, not necessarily nutrition-driven terms. Consider them with a grain of salt. Flip the package over and look at the information provided on the nutrition and ingredients label. See the following figure for a sample label and explanation of terms.

Nutrition Facts

Serving Size 1 cup (228g)
Servings Per Container about 2

Amount Per Serving

Calories 250	Calories from Fat 110

	% Daily Value*
Total Fat 12g	18%
Saturated Fat 3g	15%
Trans Fat 3g	
Cholesterol 30mg	10%
Sodium 470mg	20%
Total Carbohydrate 31g	10%
Dietary Fiber 0g	0%
Sugars 5g	
Proteins 5g	

Vitamin A	4%
Vitamin C	2%
Calcium	20%
Iron	4%

* Percent Daily Values are based on a 2,000 calorie diet.
Your Daily Values may be higher or lower depending on
your calorie needs:

	Calories:	2,000	2,500
Total Fat	Less than	65g	80g
Saturated Fat	Less than	20g	25g
Cholesterol	Less than	300mg	300mg
Sodium	Less than	2,400mg	2,400mg
Total Carbohydrate		300g	375g
Dietary Fiber		25g	30g

For educational purposes only. This label does not meet the labeling
requirements described in 21 CFR 101.9.

① Serving Size
This section is the basis for determining number of calories, amount of each nutrient, and %DVs of a food. Use it to compare a serving size to how much you actually eat. Serving sizes are given in familiar units, such as cups or pieces, followed by the metric amount, e.g., number of grams.

② Amount of Calories
If you want to manage your weight (lose, gain, or maintain), this section is especially helpful. The amount of calories is listed on the left side. The right side shows how many calories in one serving come from fat. In this example, there are 250 calories, 110 of which come from fat. The key is to balance how many calories you eat with how many calories your body uses. *Tip: Remember that a product that's fat-free isn't necessarily calorie-free.*

③ Limit these Nutrients
Eating too much total fat (including saturated fat and trans fat), cholesterol, or sodium may increase your risk of certain chronic diseases, such as heart disease, some cancers, or high blood pressure. The goal is to stay below 100%DV for each of these nutrients per day.

④ Get Enough of these Nutrients
Americans often don't get enough dietary fiber, vitamin A, vitamin C, calcium, and iron in their diets. Eating enough of these nutrients may improve your health and help reduce the risk of some diseases and conditions.

⑤ Percent (%) Daily Value
This section tells you whether the nutrients (total fat, sodium, dietary fiber, etc.) in one serving of food contribute a little or a lot to your total daily diet.

The %DVs are based on a 2,000-calorie diet. Each listed nutrient is based on 100% of the recommended amounts for that nutrient. For example, 18% for total fat means that one serving furnishes 18% of the total amount of fat that you could eat in a day and stay within public health recommendations. Use the Quick Guide to Percent DV (%DV): 5%DV or less is low and 20%DV or more is high.

⑥ Footnote with Daily Values (DVs)
The footnote provides information about the DVs for important nutrients, including fats, sodium and fiber. The DVs are listed for people who eat 2,000 or 2,500 calories each day.

– The amounts for total fat, saturated fat, cholesterol, and sodium are maximum amounts. That means you should try to stay below the amounts listed.

Source: U.S. Food and Drug Administration, Nutrition Facts Label High-resolution Images for Print Media, Last updated 08/14/2015.
http://www.fda.gov/Food/IngredientsPackagingLabeling/LabelingNutrition/ucml14155.htm.

At the writing of this book, the FDA is proposing updates to make serving sizes and nutrition science information more understandable.

The label provides helpful detail for those counting or tracking macronutrients. My personal preference and recommendation to clients are to read the ingredients list on packaged and restaurant foods. The list of ingredients can be quite eye opening, and a quick scan provides enough information to determine if the food is a fit for your earthly temple.

Consider the ingredients list for McDonald's french fries. One might think french fries are made from potatoes, oil, and salt. Not at Mickey D's.

Ingredients in McDonald's World Famous Fries
Source: www.mcdonalds.com, accessed 12/27/15

Potatoes, Vegetable Oil (Canola Oil, Soybean Oil, Hydrogenated Soybean Oil, Natural Beef Flavor [Wheat and Milk Derivatives]*, Citric Acid [Preservative]), Dextrose, Sodium Acid Pyrophosphate (Maintain Color), Salt. Prepared in Vegetable Oil (Canola Oil, Corn Oil, Soybean Oil, Hydrogenated Soybean Oil) with TBHQ and Citric Acid to preserve freshness of the oil and Dimethylpolysiloxane to reduce oil splatter when cooking.
CONTAINS: WHEAT AND MILK

*Natural beef flavor contains hydrolyzed wheat and hydrolyzed milk as starting ingredients.

So, McDonald's fries contain milk, wheat, dextrose (a form of sugar made from corn), the chemical preservative tertiary butylhydroquinone (TBHQ), and the polymer of silicone dimethylpolysiloxane. One gram of TBHQ can cause nausea, vomiting, and delirium, and five grams of TBHQ can kill you. Dimethylpolysiloxane is used in cosmetics and Silly Putty.

If it makes you feel better, the amount of these substances is under the safe limit imposed by the FDA. *It doesn't make me feel better. I don't put that junk in my temple.*

Looking at the ingredients list makes food selection relatively easy. Consider the choices of two snack foods: Baked Flaming Hot Cheetos or SmartFood Cheddar Popcorn.

The "Baked" labeling on the Cheetos may sway folks to think it is the healthier, fitter choice. But peep the ingredients list on the next page.

Baked Flaming Hot Cheetos Ingredients	SmartFood Cheddar Popcorn Ingredients
Enriched Corn Meal, (Corn Meal, Ferrous Sulfate, Niacin, Thiamin Mononitrate, Riboflavin, and Folic Acid), Vegetable Oil (Corn, Canola, and/or Sunflower Oil), Salt, Sea Minerals (Calcium Carbonate and Magnesium Carbonate), Sugar, Monosodium Glutamate, Yeast Extract, Citric Acid, Artificial Color (Red 40 Lake, Yellow 6 Lake, Yellow 6, Yellow 5), Hydrolyzed Corn Protein, Onion Powder, Cheddar Cheese (Milk, Cheese Cultures, Salt, Enzymes), Whey, Maltodextrin (Made from Corn), Whey Protein Concentrate, Garlic Powder, Buttermilk, Natural Flavor, Sodium Diacetate, Lactic Acid, Disodium Inosinate, Disodium Guanylate, and Skim Milk. Contains Milk Ingredients	Popcorn, Vegetable Oil (Corn, Canola, and/or Sunflower Oil), Cheddar Cheese (Milk, Cheese Cultures, Salt, Enzymes), Whey, Buttermilk, and Salt. Contains Milk Ingredients.

Baked Flaming Hot Cheetos contain a boatload more additives and artificial ingredients than the cheddar popcorn. Our fearfully and wonderfully made bodies do not respond well to junk. The popcorn (the one without any reduced fat claims) is a better choice.

KISS (Keep It Simple Saint) for Faithfully Fit Eating

- Choose real whole foods. Natural foods have simple ingredient lists. For example, the ingredients list for a banana is banana. Wonderful snack choice!
- When possible, don't rely on restaurants or manufacturing plants to prepare your food. You can do it. *You can!*
- In selecting packaged food, if the ingredients list is a paragraph and reads like a Chem101 text with hard-to-pronounce words, numbers, and acronyms—pass. That item is on Team Too Much. Your body deserves better.

Examine Thyself

1. Review the list of not-so-healthy traditional foods you eat regularly on page 170.

    Do you value tradition more than your health?

    ❑ Yes   ❑ No   ❑ Sometimes

    If you checked yes, pray about this and move to Number 2.

    On your list, place an X by the food if the regular consumption of that item means more to you than your weight loss goals.

    At this point, foods without an X are foods you are willing to adjust. Bravo on your willingness to change! In the space below, list changes with these foods you can make to support weight loss and physical stewardship. *(Examples: Substitutions, different preparations, reduced frequency or consumption.)*

2. Take this book to your pantry or cabinet. Select 12 packaged items you eat regularly. Read the ingredients label and determine if this food is a fit for your increasingly fit body. If the answer is no and you are led to do so, dump it in the trash.

Item	Is it a keeper?
1.	❏ Yes ❏ No
2.	❏ Yes ❏ No
3.	❏ Yes ❏ No
4.	❏ Yes ❏ No
5.	❏ Yes ❏ No
6.	❏ Yes ❏ No
7.	❏ Yes ❏ No
8.	❏ Yes ❏ No
9.	❏ Yes ❏ No
10.	❏ Yes ❏ No
11.	❏ Yes ❏ No
12.	❏ Yes ❏ No

Recipe Remake - Nettye's Nix the Mix Cornbread

Traditional Old School Soul Food Cornbread contains lard or shortening and significant amounts of sugar. Contemporary cornbread (from a box) is also packed with unhealthy ingredients (See ingredients of beloved Jiffy Cornbread Mix below). Since my family eats cornbread a few days per week, I created this recipe. Part of my Nix the Mix collection, it is a tasty, healthier version that is almost as fast as the box preparation.
Makes one pan cornbread - 8-12 servings

Ingredients:
1 cup unbleached flour (*manufacturers use chemicals to whiten bleached flour*)
1 cup corn meal
3 ½ teaspoons baking powder
¾ teaspoon salt
Up to ¼ cup sugar (I use 2 tablespoons sugar or ¼ cup honey)
1 egg, lightly beaten
¼ cup + 1 Tablespoon oil (canola or vegetable)
1 cup milk of choice (I use 2% milk, or unsweetened almond milk)

Instructions:
Preheat oven to 375 degrees. Place cast iron skillet with 1 tablespoon oil in the oven while preheating so the skillet and oil get hot.

Mix dry ingredients (flour, corn meal, baking powder, salt and granulated sugar) in a bowl until items are well combined.

Add egg, oil, and milk (and honey if used for sweetener instead of sugar). Stir until dry ingredients are incorporated. Do not over mix.

Pour batter into hot skillet and bake 15-20 minutes or until the cornbread is set and slightly browned on the edges.

Cool on a wire rack and enjoy.

This recipe is very flexible. If you like sweet cornbread, add more sugar. If you like cornbread with a cakier texture, increase the amount of flour and reduce and reduce the amount of cornmeal. If you like a mealier cornbread, increase the amount of cornmeal and reduce the amount of flour. Just make sure the flour and cornmeal combined equals 2 cups. If you don't have a cast-iron skillet, use a 9" round pan or muffin tin. Adjust baking time to fit.

Jiffy Cornbread Mix Ingredients

Wheat Flour, Degerminated Yellow Corn Meal, Sugar, Animal Shortening (contains one or more of the following: Lard, Hydrogenated Lard, Partially Hydrogenated Lard), contains less than 2 of each of the following: Baking Soda, Sodium Acid Pyrophosphate, Monocalcium Phosphate, Salt, Wheat Starch, Niacin, Reduced Iron, BHT Preservative, Tocopherol Preservative, Citric Acid Preservative, BHA Preservative, Tricalcium Phosphate, Thiamine Mononitrate, Riboflavin, Folic Acid, Silicon Dioxide.   Source: www.jiffymix.com, accessed December 27, 2015

Recipe Remake - Crawfish Pasta

You can't beat a good recipe remake—recipes of those good-to-us foods, made over to be better-for-us. Here is my favorite lightened version of Crawfish Pasta adapted from a recipe found in Cooking Light *magazine. I've served this several times to native Louisianans who don't do "diet food." Each time it was a hit.*

Makes approximately 6 1-cup servings

Ingredients:
1 tablespoon olive oil
2 cups onion, finely chopped
1 cup green bell pepper, finely chopped
½ cup celery, finely chopped
3 garlic cloves, minced
¼ cup unbleached flour
1 (12-ounce) can evaporated skim milk

1 cup sharp 2% cheddar cheese
¼ cup grated parmesan cheese
1-pound bag peeled crawfish tails, thawed
¼ - ½ teaspoon creole salt
¼ teaspoon cayenne pepper
¼ teaspoon black pepper

1 (10-ounce) can mild tomatoes with chilies, undrained (I like Rotel)
8 ounces whole-wheat pasta of choice (I like fettuccine - cook enough to yield 4 cups cooked pasta)

Instructions:
Preheat oven to 350.

Bring a stockpot of water to a boil. Stir in some salt and the pasta. Boil until pasta is al dente (about 8-10 minutes).

While pasta is boiling, heat olive oil in a large skillet and sauté chopped onion, bell pepper, and celery until onion is transparent (4 minutes).

Add garlic, stir, and cook another minute until fragrant.

Add flour and cook ~2 minutes, stirring constantly. Try not to brown the flour; you just want to cook out the floury taste.

Stir in canned milk and tomatoes with green chilies. Cook 6-7 minutes or until the mixture thickens to coat the back of a spoon.

Drain pasta and add it to the skillet with the cheeses, crawfish tails, salt, and peppers. Adjust salt and peppers to taste.

Spoon mixture into a 13 x 9-inch baking dish and bake for 25 minutes until bubbly.

Crawfish, aka crayfish, crawdads, or mudbugs, are freshwater crustaceans that look like tiny lobsters. If unavailable, substitute shrimp, cooked chicken (for non-seafood version) or a mix of sautéed mushrooms (for a vegetarian version).

Recipe Remake - Momma's Egg Custard Pie

This is my beautiful Momma.

The recipe that follows is a remake of her delectable egg custard pie.

The sweetest food memories of my childhood involve Momma's hand cranked homemade vanilla ice cream (that would put Blue Bell to shame) and this pie. I'm not yet able to make her ice cream, but Momma's pie is on the dessert table at my home every holiday. The pie is silky and delicately flavored. My husband adores it, and our baby girl would eat an entire pie if allowed. I hope you will enjoy it too.

Ingredients:

1 Tablespoon softened butter
2 Tablespoons unbleached flour
½ - ¾ cup granulated sugar
½ Tablespoon ground cinnamon
Pinch of salt

2 eggs
1 ¼ cup 2% milk
1 Tablespoon vanilla extract
1-9" pie crust (butter based)

Instructions:

Preheat oven to 400 degrees.

In a mixer, combine butter, flour, sugar, salt and cinnamon. Mix until smooth.

Add eggs and vanilla. Mix to combine. Turn mixer to low. Slowly pour in milk. Mix ingredients well.

Pour into pie crust. Be sure to scrape and stir the mixing bowl with a spoon to make sure you get all the goodness off the bottom.

Bake for 10 minutes. Reduce oven to 350 degrees and continue to bake until pie is set (40-45 minutes). Remove from oven and allow pie to cool and set. Serve warm or refrigerate and serve cold.

Momma's original recipe is rich. My changes, i.e. reduction of sugar, butter and use of low-fat milk lighten it a bit without sacrificing flavor. (I typically use a little shy of ½ cup sugar.)
To make the pie diabetic friendly, replace up to half the total amount sugar used with Splenda granulated sugar. Example: instead of ¾ cup granulated sugar, use 3/8 cup granulated sugar and 3/8 cup Splenda granulated sugar.

Praction (Prayer - Action)

Journal your thoughts, prayer, and plan of action from this section.

HONOR
GOD

CHAPTER 10

Embrace the Fast

Fasting from any nourishment, activity, involvement or pursuit—for any season—sets the stage for God to appear."
Dan B. Allender

FIRST, LET ME BE clear—in no way, shape, form, or fashion do I suggest anyone fast to lose weight.

I do, however, strongly encourage fasting to increase spiritual strength.

Fasting is a tremendously powerful spiritual discipline that deepens intimacy with God.

Fasting tunes out the loud call and distracting noise of the flesh and allows us to better hear and heed the voice of the Holy Spirit. By surrendering our bodies, eyes can be opened, attitudes and appetites can be changed, and strongholds can be broken.

Moses fasted on Mount Sinai before receiving the Ten Commandments (Exodus 34:28).

Running from Jezebel, afraid, weary, and ready to give up, Elijah fasted on the long journey to Horeb, after which the Lord appeared and gave him clear direction (1 Kings 19:8-16).

Esther fasted and entreated the Jews in Susa to fast with her before she went before the king to beg mercy for her people (Esther 4:15-16).

David fasted as he pleaded for the life of his son (2 Samuel 12:15-17).

After repenting, all the people of Ninevah fasted (Jonah 3:5).

The old widow and prophet Anna regularly fasted in the temple where she beheld young Jesus (Luke 2:36-37).

After meeting Jesus on the road to Damascus, Paul fasted (Acts 9:3-9).

In the wilderness, before beginning His public ministry, our Lord and Savior fasted (Matthew 4:1-2).

Notice a pattern in this handful of biblical examples. While the situations differ, all were difficult. Here we see times of stress, uncertainty, danger, temptation, or trouble, states of physical, spiritual, and/or emotional weakness. In my mind's eye, when I attempt to step into scripture, putting myself in each of these situations, I imagine they were unsure what would happen, where to go, or what to do. These examples show a response of submission and seeking God that included the spiritual discipline of fasting and prayer. God responded.

When in need, fasting and prayer preceded blessing.

When in danger, fasting and prayer prompted protection.

When uncertain, fasting and prayer paved the way for clarity and answers.

When tempted, fasting and prayer prepared them to receive their call.

Shifting the application of God's Word from a lens exploring their lives to a mirror examining my life, looking back to my actions and reactions via the lens of God's Word—I saw a different pattern.

Instead of turning immediately to God, I reflexively turned first to food.

Granted, my circumstances have not been as dire (thanks be to God). Yet in times of stress, uncertainty, temptation, or trial, in states of physical, spiritual, and/or emotional weakness, when I was unsure what would happen, where to go, or what to do, my first response was to medicate the discomfort.

Instead of turning immediately to God, I reflexively turned first to food.

Emotional eaters—holler if you hear me.

Stressed out! *I'd eat.*

Tired! *I'd eat.*

Afraid, confused, lonely, overwhelmed! I'd eat, eat, eat, and eat some more.

It was my first response. My automatic outreach. At that moment, I moved to feel better in body before I gave attention to Spirit. I automatically sought a natural salve to a need that required supernatural help.

A question begs for consideration. In the quickness to answer the call of the flesh, do we miss more important calls from God?

Seven years ago in an Introduction to Old Testament class, a discussion took place about stewardship in the body of Christ. New Orleans Theological Seminary professor Pastor Dave recommended a few books on fasting, stating if believers truly understood the power of fasting and embraced it is a spiritual discipline, the effect on our individual lives and resulting impact in our churches, communities, and society would be astounding.

I found the statement to be a bit extreme. Mention stewardship and the immediate connection in my mind was tithing. Tithing is taught—a lot—and a 10 percent level of giving tends to be fair and comfortable. But fasting? I had little knowledge, less personal experience, and to be honest—I didn't connect fasting with stewardship. I connected it with suffering, suffering that was not needed or required.

I suspect my point of view is common, since fasting is not emphasized in many churches today.

Fasting was embraced and commonly practiced by the early church, a period where the church experienced significant growth and strength in spite of opposition and persecution. With time, acceptance of the practice of fasting declined. By the dark Middle Ages, the view of fasting dimmed to an extreme act of asceticism.[59] It was something for priests, monks, or fanatics only. Many believers today maintain that "extreme" perspective.

In my 30-plus years as a proud Baptist, I've heard little teaching, preaching, emphasis, or even encouragement of fasting. It has been said that we are a denomination more active in feasting than fasting. Baptists are not alone. Truth be told, many churches regularly promote and participate in gluttony and either overlook fasting or deem it a fringe practice.

Find this statement far-fetched?

Observe the next church potluck, banquet, luncheon, or other church-related gathering that involves food. There will be some gluttony going on.

Joyful gluttony.

Joke and laugh and tell-folks-all-about-how-much-you-overate gluttony. It just won't be labeled as such. It will be called good fellowship.

Next compare the occurrences of "good fellowship" against the times fasting has been explored in the preached Word, Bible studies, church school lessons, prayer meetings, or other ministry events.

Feast over fast, time and time again.

This is not an indictment of any denomination or individuals in *Fasting* the body of Christ. It is, however, an indication *can break* of the stronghold food has in the lives of far too *strongholds!* many Christians.

But fasting can break strongholds!

Fasting Defined

Simply defined, Christian fasting is prayer-full abstinence from food and/or drink for spiritual purposes. Intricately connected with prayer, fasting deepens our connection to God.

In the Old Testament, we see prayer and fasting done as acts of repentance, as mourning, and as calls for God's presence and His hand in their given situations. In New Testament times, fasting moved beyond legalism to a way to imitate Christ.

God does not require us to fast. It is a voluntary choice. In his book *The Fasting Edge*, Jentezen Franklin explains,

It is a vow you choose to make to pursue God on a deeper level. The entire time that you are on a fast, you are acknowledging God. When you are feeling hungry, empty, and weak, you connect with

God without all the clutter. In that way, fasting is a time vow. It is also a discipline vow. Fasting, especially a longer fast, strengthens your character in every area of your life.[60]

Scripture details three forms of fasting:

1. Absolute fasts
2. Liquid fasts
3. Partials fasts

Absolute fasts involve abstaining from all food and liquids for a period. Examples in scripture include Moses' 40-day fast on Mount Sinai (Exodus 34:28), Queen Esther and the Jews' three-day fast before she went to address the king (Esther 4:15-16) and the Apostle Paul's three-day fast after meeting Jesus on the road to Damascus (Acts 9:9).

Absolute fasts lasting an extended period are often called supernatural absolute fasts because it is a miracle to live more than three days without water or 21 days without food. Due to their taxing nature, absolute fasts should only be undertaken if your health is good and you have complete clarity and confidence that the Holy Spirit is directing you to this task.

Liquid fasts involve abstaining from food and consuming only liquids for a period. Water and fruit and vegetable juices are the liquids typically consumed on this fast. While challenging, liquid fasts are not as dangerous as absolute fasts, since the body gets needed liquids and some nutrition.

Partial fasts involve abstaining from groups of food or drink for a period. Popular examples in scripture are Daniel's 10-day and 21-day fasts (Daniel 1:12-15 and 10:2-3). Other variations of the partial fasts are time-based instead of food or beverage based, for example, abstaining from food or drink certain hours of the day. Many believers with medical considerations choose this fast.

In addition to types of fasts, fasting has two extent categories, individual or corporate. Individual fasts involve just God and the believer and are often conducted in private (Matthew 6:16-18). Corporate fasts involve God and a group of believers. The group can be a family, church family, or another group of people connected for a spiritual purpose. Some church congregations enter into a corporate fast at the beginning of the New Year or to prepare for a specific call (Acts 14:23).

If food is a stronghold in your life, go to battle. Take it to God in prayer, and if led to fast, fast. Sacrifice the control food has over you in devotion and dedication to God and see where the Holy Spirit leads.

Praction (Prayer - Action)

Journal your thoughts, prayer, and plan of action from this section.

CHAPTER 11

Willpower. Want Power. God's Power

Finally, be strong in the Lord and in his mighty power.
Galatians 6:10

THE PRECEDING CHAPTERS OF this book outline philosophies and strategies to manage weight and health. Hopefully, you have identified areas of strength and health habits that need some strengthening. I also hope you have gained helpful information, enabling the creation of your Faithfully Fit Food Philosophy and defining other essential steps to your best body. Moreover, I pray God's desire that you be well and in good health has focused your mind and touched your heart; you are excited and ready to live your God-given potential.

The information and adjustments outlined are not complex or overly involved. Actually, the steps are relatively easy. Taking the steps—consistently—now, that can be hard.

Nike says, "Just do it." But how? How do we start and maintain the focus and energy to do what we should do? What do we need not to get weary in doing well for our temples?

I suggest three things are required. Willpower, want power, and God's power.

Willpower

The Merriam-Webster dictionary defines willpower as:

> *the ability to control yourself : strong determination that allows you to do something difficult (such as to lose weight or quit smoking)*

Listed synonyms include: restraint, self-command, self-containment, self-control, self-discipline, self-government, self-mastery, self-possession, and self-restraint.

It is interesting that the dictionary includes weight loss in the definition of willpower. Certainly it takes willpower to shed pounds and keep them off.

Willpower is more closely tied to energy than will, specifically the blood glucose available to our brain. Scientific study confirms that when blood glucose levels are high, willpower, or self-control, is high. The converse is also true—when blood glucose levels dip, willpower takes a dive.

No one has infinite willpower. It is a limited resource that ebbs and flows during the day. The functioning of willpower has been compared to a muscle that gets tired when overworked. Typically, willpower is strongest in the morning, after the brain has had a night's rest. Throughout the day we make decisions, solve problems, fight temptations and control emotions—and our willpower depletes. Now add the aforementioned fluctuations of blood glucose and we see why willpower can go to pot. Let's say you set a goal to control your temper or tongue. Willpower can help you keep the lips zipped and anger in check. What happens to that control when you are dog tired, hungry, and someone cuts you off in traffic or the wrong person says the wrong thing? *Somebody better watch out!*

Watch how this can affect weight loss efforts:

- Morning exercisers tend to be more consistent than those who exercise later in the day (even though physical energy is highest in early afternoon).

- Eating choices are typically healthier earlier in the day vs. late at night. (Those late-night raids of the pantry are partly due to the need for brain energy.)

- According to the American Psychological Association, 43 percent of Americans report overeating to manage stress.[61] (Stress gives willpower a beat down.)

Leverage willpower facts to sustain positive action and boost motivation.

Those actions critical to your success that don't get done? Give them laser focus and action early in the day when willpower is highest. Example: A person trying to drink more water, but unable to get it in each day, may set out to drink three-fourths of the daily goal before 2 p.m.

Fall to certain temptations every evening? Close the door of opportunity when you know willpower is weakest. Example: Healthy eating goes to pot every night? Stop all eating at a certain time. "Close" the kitchen after dinner. Or go to sleep.

Willpower is helpful but not enough. Don't rely on it alone. We need and have more juice to get and keep us going.

Want power

While willpower is seated primarily in the brain, I suggest want power resides in our head, heart, and flesh.

When we want something—really want something—it occupies our thoughts. It manifests as a desire of our heart. And some wants (both helpful and harmful) are bred from the call of the flesh.

We have seen the power of want:

- The toddler who sees his favorite treat on a shelf above his reach and becomes Baby MacGyver to get it.
- The drug addict craving a fix.
- The financially strapped college student who knows education prepares her path to success.
- The woman who wants her Boo to put a ring on it.

Want power drives us. It can boost energy, unlock ingenuity, and enable super-creative problem-solving. Want power moves folks to do what needs to be done to get what they want.

> ^{2}*Now there is in Jerusalem near the Sheep Gate a pool, which in Aramaic is called Bethesda and which is surrounded by five covered colonnades. ^{3}Here a great number of disabled people used to lie—the blind, the lame, the paralyzed. ^{5}One who was there had been an invalid for thirty-eight years. ^{6}When Jesus saw him lying there and learned that he had been in this condition for a long time, he asked him, "Do you want to get well?"*
>
> ^{7}*"Sir," the invalid replied, "I have no one to help me into the pool when the water is stirred. While I am trying to get in, someone else goes down ahead of me."*
>
> ^{8}*Then Jesus said to him, "Get up! Pick up your mat and walk." ^{9}At once the man was cured; he picked up his mat and walked.* John 5:2-9 NIV

Jesus traveled to Jerusalem for a Jewish festival and stopped at the pool by the Sheep Gate north of the temple area. The Bethesda pool was special. Healing came to the first person who entered the pool after the waters of the pool were disturbed. Consequently, many disabled people were by the pool, watching, waiting, and hoping for their opportunity to be healed. While many were there, scripture says Jesus engaged one, a man who had lived with an infirmity for 38 years. What followed was an intersection of divine power (Jesus) and human responsibility (the invalid).

First, Jesus asks a single question: *"Do you want to get well?"*

Jesus didn't ask who he was. Jesus didn't inquire about his belief or faith. The question Jesus asked addressed the condition of the invalid's heart. *"Do you want to get well?"*

Place yourself in this encounter and hear Jesus ask you the same. *"Do you want to get well?"*

Do you **want** to be free from the hindrance of weight?

Do you **want** to be rid of unhealthy habits and additions?

Do you **want** to stop waiting and wishing for change?

Notice the invalid's response. What was on his heart and mind came out of his mouth. It was what he didn't have: *"I have no one to help me into the pool ..."* Challenges and past failures: *"While I am trying to get in, someone else goes down ahead of me ..."* His focus was on getting in the water, not being well.

If given space, past failures and current challenges squash the desires of our hearts and redirect our focus. Shut the negativity down!

Jesus didn't acknowledge or respond to the invalid's excuses. Jesus commanded action. Not in the manner the invalid had tried before. Jesus didn't tell him to go down in the water.

Jesus told the invalid to do something he thought he could not do: *"Get up!"*

Jesus told the invalid to remove the provision for relapse: *"Pick up your mat ..."*

Jesus told the invalid to step into his healing: *"... and walk."*

This miracle, this long-awaited healing, this awesome display of Jesus' power accessed through faithful human action and obedience started with *"Do you want to get well?"*

Stop here and prayerfully contemplate. What do I want?

Record on this page what is impressed on your heart. Put it in a note on your phone. Write it on a card and post it on your bathroom mirror, on your desk at work, on the door of your refrigerator, and in your pantry. Place it where you will see it often. Use it to focus your thoughts, refresh your heart, and motivate action.

I want

Most importantly, in prayer, tell God what you want regarding your weight and health. Lay it all out before Him. Listen for His will and His command. Then act.

God's Power

Willpower is seated primarily in the brain. It helps us do what we need to do, but willpower is limited.

Want power resides in our head, heart, and flesh. It can motivate action, but our desires can be diluted or misdirected.

Willpower and want power are needed. But for permanent positive change, we need the power of God. God's power is unlimited. It is immutable. It is perfect. And we have so graciously been given access via the indwelling presence of the Holy Spirit.

God does not want us to tackle weight or any other challenge before us alone.

Let these scriptures speak to your soul.

"Not by might nor by power, but by my Spirit," says the Lord Almighty. Zechariah 4:6

"I am the vine; you are the branches. If you remain in me and I in you, you will bear much fruit; apart from me you can do nothing." John 15:5

I can do all this through him who gives me strength. Philippians 4:13

I lift up my eyes to the mountains—
*   where does my help come from?*
² My help comes from the Lord,
*   the Maker of heaven and earth.*
Psalm 121:1-2

But he said to me, "My grace is sufficient for you, for my power is made perfect in weakness." ... For when I am weak, then I am strong. 2 Corinthians 12:9-10

So, if you think you are standing firm, be careful that you don't fall!
¹³ No temptation has overtaken you except what is common to mankind. And God is faithful; he will not let you be tempted beyond what you can bear. But when you are tempted, he will also provide a way out so that you can endure it. 1 Corinthians 10:12-13

"With man this is impossible, but with God all things are possible." Matthew 19:26

Finally, be strong in the Lord and in his mighty power. Ephesians 6:10

God is the key, the core, the reason, our strength. He is the source of everything we need. Apart from God we can do nothing.

Surrender your challenges.

Honor Him with your choices.

Do your part so His desire that you prosper and be in good health manifests in your life.

Now unto him that is able to do exceeding abundantly above all that we ask or think, according to the power that worketh in us, Unto him be glory in the church by Christ Jesus throughout all ages, world without end. Amen.[62]

Praction (Prayer - Action)

Journal your thoughts, prayer, and plan of action from this section.

CHAPTER 12

Path to Salvation

For what shall it profit a man, if he shall gain the whole world,
and lose his own soul?
Mark 8:36 KJV

GOD DESIRES NOT ONLY that you be healthy. Far more important than that, our Creator desires for you to be whole. Complete. Connected to Him.

Here is the most important self-examination question in this book—and in all of life.

Are you saved?

The question is not "Are you a church member?" Nor is it "Are you a good person?"

I'm asking, are you whole? Are you complete? Are you connected to God?

If you are not, and you want to be, you can be. Right now.

Salvation and security are available to you, and God's plan is simple.

Admit

First beloved, you must recognize and admit that you are a sinner in need of a savior. We all are.

> *As it is written: "There is no one righteous, not even one."* Romans 3:10

> *For all have sinned and fall short of the glory of God.* Romans 3:23

Sin means missing the mark defined by God. It is a refusal to acknowledge God's authority over our lives. Sin includes doing "wrong" as well as failure to do things that are "right." Sin is not restricted to action; it affects our mind and the condition of our hearts. We all have thoughts, urges, words, and actions that are harmful, hurtful, unloving, and displeasing to God. Sin affects us all.

> *For the wages of sin is death, but the gift of God is eternal life in Christ Jesus our Lord.* Romans 6:23

The result of sin is spiritual death—separation from God. God loves the world and desires a personal relationship with each person. He is also holy, perfect, and righteous, and sin is contrary to His nature.

Admitting sin is the first step in the turn from sin and self towards God (repentance).

Believe

Second, believe in Jesus and accept His forgiveness for sin.

> *For God so loved the world that he gave his one and only Son, that whoever believes in him shall not perish but have eternal life.* John 3:16

> *God made him who had no sin to be sin for us, so that in him we might become the righteousness of God.* 1 Corinthians 5:21

God loves us so much that He sent His Son, Jesus Christ, to pay the price for our sins. Our sin (my sin, your sin—all of it) was laid upon Jesus. He became our substitute and provided the path to God.

Jesus died on the cross, rose from the dead, and ascended to heaven so we can be free, righteous, and whole.

Jesus did this for you.

Believe in Jesus Christ. Acknowledge who He is and accept His gift of forgiveness.

Confess and commit

Third, confess Jesus Christ as Lord and commit your life to Him.

> ... because, if you confess with your mouth that Jesus is Lord and believe in your heart that God raised him from the dead, you will be saved. [10] For with the heart one believes and is justified, and with the mouth one confesses and is saved. Romans 10:9-10

Salvation comes when you openly confess and believe in Jesus, His death, burial, and resurrection, and accept Him as Lord of your life. It is a heartfelt commitment that because "Jesus died for me, I will live for Him." When you make this confession and commitment, the Holy Spirit comes to live in you, giving you the power to change, grow, and live a life that is pleasing to God.

Are you ready to accept Jesus?

Pray

Lord, I need You. I can't make it through life on my own. I fall, I fail. I have impure thoughts and do things that are not pleasing to You. So I come with a repentant heart seeking and accepting Your forgiveness. Jesus, I believe You are the son of God, You came to earth, died on the cross for my sins and rose again. Today, I invite You into my heart and surrender my life to You. Fill me with the Holy Spirit. Help me be the person You desire.

Thank You for eternal life.

In the name of Jesus. Amen.

If your confession and commitment are sincere, you are saved. It is a promise from God.

... for, "Everyone who calls on the name of the Lord will be saved." Romans 10:13

In obedience to Christ, you should be baptized as a public testimony of your salvation.

Talk to God regularly through prayer.

Read the Bible and unite with a Bible-believing church for worship, nurturing, and growth.

To God be the glory!

Appendix A: Pulling It Together

1.   *People are destroyed for lack of knowledge.* Hosea 4:6

   Start with knowledge of self.

   Consult your medical professional to review your health status, family health history, chronic disease risks, and weight loss goals. Get his/her recommendations regarding your healthy weight, nutrition guidelines, and daily activity. Be Berean about it. Pray, research, and get additional input from qualified professionals and resources.

2.   *Write the vision; make it plain.* Habakkuk 2:2

   Craft your personal Faithfully Fit Food Philosophy (see Chapter 6). Record it below.

   _____

   _____

   _____

   _____

   _____

   _____

   _____

   _____

3. *"She clothes herself with strength, and strengthens her arms."* Proverbs 31:17

    Up your activity to work both sides of the energy balance equation (see Chapter 3).

    If needed, consult a certified fitness professional for assessment and personalized exercise programming.

4. Create small, lifelong health habits (see "Small Changes Big Results," Chapter 3).

5. *"I urge you therefore, brothers, by the mercies of God, that you present your bodies as a living sacrifice, holy, and acceptable to God, which is your reasonable service of worship."* (Romans 12:1)

    Honor God in all you do.

If you need assistance pulling your plan together, consult a certified health coach. Health coaches help clients make lifestyle and behavior changes affecting exercise, nutrition, and weight control. A faith-based approach is a critical selection criterion. This journey is for God's glory. It is unwise and ineffective to proceed without Him.

Appendix B: Scripture References by Chapter

Introduction

Jeremiah 32:27
"I am the Lord, the God of all mankind. Is anything too hard for me?

Genesis 41:15-16
[15]Pharaoh said to Joseph, "I had a dream, and no one can interpret it. But I have heard it said of you that when you hear a dream you can interpret it." [16]"I cannot do it," Joseph replied to Pharaoh, "but God will give Pharaoh the answer he desires."

Diets Do Work

1 Corinthians 6:13
You say, "Food for the stomach and the stomach for food, and God will destroy them both." The body, however, is not meant for sexual immorality but for the Lord, and the Lord for the body.

1 Corinthians 6:19-20
[19]Do you not know that your bodies are temples of the Holy Spirit, who is in you, whom you have received from God? You are not your own; [20]you were bought at a price. Therefore honor God with your bodies.

1 Corinthians 6:14
By his power God raised the Lord from the dead, and he will raise us also.

Exodus 20:3-5
[3]"You shall have no other gods before me. [4]"You shall not make for yourself an image in the form of anything in heaven above or on the earth beneath or in the waters below. [5]You shall not bow down to them or worship them; for I, the Lord your God, am a jealous God,

punishing the children for the sin of the parents to the third and fourth generation of those who hate me,"

In Search of Healthy Weight

Proverbs 15:22
Plans fail for lack of counsel,
    but with many advisers they succeed

Weight Loss Begins in Your Mind: Get Rid of Those ANTs!

Proverbs 23:7 KJV
For as he thinketh in his heart, so is he: Eat and drink, saith he to thee; but his heart is not with thee.

Philippians 4:6-8
[6]Do not be anxious about anything, but in every situation, by prayer and petition, with thanksgiving, present your requests to God. [7]And the peace of God, which transcends all understanding, will guard your hearts and your minds in Christ Jesus.
[8]Finally, brothers and sisters, whatever is true, whatever is noble, whatever is right, whatever is pure, whatever is lovely, whatever is admirable—if anything is excellent or praiseworthy—think about such things.

3 John 2
Dear friend, I pray that you may enjoy good health and that all may go well with you, even as your soul is getting along well.

Foundations for Healthy Eating

Isaiah 53:5-6 NKJV
[5]But He was wounded for our transgressions,
He was bruised for our iniquities;
The chastisement for our peace was upon Him,
And by His stripes we are healed.

[6]All we like sheep have gone astray;
We have turned, every one, to his own way;
And the Lord has laid on Him the iniquity of us all.

Proverbs 27:17
Iron sharpens iron, so one man sharpens another.

Matthew 18:15-17
[15]"If your brother or sister sins, go and point out their fault, just between the two of you. If they listen to you, you have won them over. [16]But if they will not listen, take one or two others along, so that 'every matter may be established by the testimony of two or three witnesses.' [17]If they still refuse to listen, tell it to the church; and if they refuse to listen even to the church, treat them as you would a pagan or a tax collector.

Matthew 7:1-5
[1]"Do not judge, or you too will be judged. [2]For in the same way you judge others, you will be judged, and with the measure you use, it will be measured to you.
[3]"Why do you look at the speck of sawdust in your brother's eye and pay no attention to the plank in your own eye? [4]How can you say to your brother, 'Let me take the speck out of your eye,' when all the time there is a plank in your own eye? [5]You hypocrite, first take the plank out of your own eye, and then you will see clearly to remove the speck from your brother's eye.

Eat Less Meat

Genesis 1:27-29
[27]So God created mankind in his own image, in the image of God he created them; male and female he created them. [28]God blessed them and said to them, "Be fruitful and increase in number; fill the earth and subdue it. Rule over the fish in the sea and the birds in the sky and over every living creature that moves on the ground." [29]Then God said, "I give you every seed-bearing plant on the face of the whole earth and every tree that has fruit with seed in it. They will be yours for food."

Genesis 9:1-3
[1]Then God blessed Noah and his sons, saying to them, "Be fruitful and increase in number and fill the earth. [2]The fear and dread of you will fall on all the beasts of the earth, and on all the birds in the sky, on every creature that moves along the ground, and on all the fish in the

sea; they are given into your hands. ³Everything that lives and moves about will be food for you. Just as I gave you the green plants, I now give you everything."

Luke 12:47-48
⁴⁷"The servant who knows the master's will and does not get ready or does not do what the master wants will be beaten with many blows. ⁴⁸But the one who does not know and does things deserving punishment will be beaten with few blows. From everyone who has been given much, much will be demanded; and from the one who has been entrusted with much, much more will be asked.

Adopt a Food Philosophy

1 Corinthians 10:23, 31
"I have the right to do anything," you say—but not everything is beneficial. "I have the right to do anything"—but not everything is constructive. ³¹So whether you eat or drink or whatever you do, do it all for the glory of God.

Experience Food

Ephesians 5:18
Do not get drunk on wine, which leads to debauchery. Instead, be filled with the Spirit,

Proverbs 20:1
Wine is a mocker and beer a brawler; whoever is led astray by them is not wise.

1 Timothy 5:23
Stop drinking only water, and use a little wine because of your stomach and your frequent illnesses.

John 2:1-11
On the third day a wedding took place at Cana in Galilee. Jesus' mother was there, ²and Jesus and his disciples had also been invited to the wedding. ³When the wine was gone, Jesus' mother said to him, "They have no more wine."
⁴"Woman, why do you involve me?" Jesus replied. "My hour has not yet come."
⁵His mother said to the servants, "Do whatever he tells you."

[6]Nearby stood six stone water jars, the kind used by the Jews for ceremonial washing, each holding from twenty to thirty gallons.
[7]Jesus said to the servants, "Fill the jars with water"; so they filled them to the brim.
[8]Then he told them, "Now draw some out and take it to the master of the banquet."They did so, [9]and the master of the banquet tasted the water that had been turned into wine. He did not realize where it had come from, though the servants who had drawn the water knew. Then he called the bridegroom aside [10]and said, "Everyone brings out the choice wine first and then the cheaper wine after the guests have had too much to drink; but you have saved the best till now."
[11]What Jesus did here in Cana of Galilee was the first of the signs through which he revealed his glory; and his disciples believed in him.

Embrace the Fast

Exodus 34:28
And he was there with the Lord forty days and forty nights; he did neither eat bread, nor drink water. And he wrote upon the tables the words of the covenant, the ten commandments.

1 Kings 19:8-16
[8]So he got up and ate and drank. Strengthened by that food, he traveled forty days and forty nights until he reached Horeb, the mountain of God. [9]There he went into a cave and spent the night.
The Lord Appears to Elijah
And the word of the Lord came to him: "What are you doing here, Elijah?" [10]He replied, "I have been very zealous for the Lord God Almighty. The Israelites have rejected your covenant, torn down your altars, and put your prophets to death with the sword. I am the only one left, and now they are trying to kill me too."
[11]The Lord said, "Go out and stand on the mountain in the presence of the Lord, for the Lord is about to pass by."
Then a great and powerful wind tore the mountains apart and shattered the rocks before the Lord, but the Lord was not in the wind. After the wind there was an earthquake, but the Lord was not in the earthquake. [12]After the earthquake came a fire, but the Lord was not in the fire. And after the fire came a gentle whisper. [13]When Elijah

heard it, he pulled his cloak over his face and went out and stood at the mouth of the cave.

Then a voice said to him, "What are you doing here, Elijah?"

[14]He replied, "I have been very zealous for the Lord God Almighty. The Israelites have rejected your covenant, torn down your altars, and put your prophets to death with the sword. I am the only one left, and now they are trying to kill me too."

[15]The Lord said to him, "Go back the way you came, and go to the Desert of Damascus. When you get there, anoint Hazael king over Aram. [16]Also, anoint Jehu son of Nimshi king over Israel, and anoint Elisha son of Shaphat from Abel Meholah to succeed you as prophet.

Esther 4:15-16

[15]Then Esther sent this reply to Mordecai: [16]"Go, gather together all the Jews who are in Susa, and fast for me. Do not eat or drink for three days, night or day. I and my attendants will fast as you do. When this is done, I will go to the king, even though it is against the law. And if I perish, I perish."

2 Samuel 12:15-17

[15]After Nathan had gone home, the Lord struck the child that Uriah's wife had borne to David, and he became ill. [16]David pleaded with God for the child. He fasted and spent the nights lying in sackcloth[b] on the ground. [17]The elders of his household stood beside him to get him up from the ground, but he refused, and he would not eat any food with them.

Jonah 3:5

The Ninevites believed God. A fast was proclaimed, and all of them, from the greatest to the least, put on sackcloth.

Luke 2:36-38

[36]There was also a prophet, Anna, the daughter of Penuel, of the tribe of Asher. She was very old; she had lived with her husband seven years after her marriage, [37]and then was a widow until she was eighty-four. She never left the temple but worshiped night and day, fasting and praying. [38]Coming up to them at that very moment, she gave thanks to God and spoke about the child to all who were looking forward to the redemption of Jerusalem.

Acts 9:3-9

[3]As he neared Damascus on his journey, suddenly a light from heaven flashed around him. [4]He fell to the ground and heard a voice say to him, "Saul, Saul, why do you persecute me?" [5]"Who are you, Lord?" Saul asked. "I am Jesus, whom you are persecuting," he replied. [6]"Now get up and go into the city, and you will be told what you must do." [7]The men traveling with Saul stood there speechless; they heard the sound but did not see anyone. [8]Saul got up from the ground, but when he opened his eyes he could see nothing. So they led him by the hand into Damascus. [9]For three days he was blind, and did not eat or drink anything.

Matthew 4:1-2
Then Jesus was led by the Spirit into the wilderness to be tempted by the devil. [2]After fasting forty days and forty nights, he was hungry.

Daniel 1:12-15
[12]"Please test your servants for ten days: Give us nothing but vegetables to eat and water to drink. [13]Then compare our appearance with that of the young men who eat the royal food, and treat your servants in accordance with what you see." [14]So he agreed to this and tested them for ten days. [15]At the end of the ten days they looked healthier and better nourished than any of the young men who ate the royal food.

Daniel 10:2-3
[2]At that time I, Daniel, mourned for three weeks. [3]I ate no choice food; no meat or wine touched my lips; and I used no lotions at all until the three weeks were over.

Matthew 6:16-18
[16]"When you fast, do not look somber as the hypocrites do, for they disfigure their faces to show others they are fasting. Truly I tell you, they have received their reward in full. [17]But when you fast, put oil on your head and wash your face, [18]so that it will not be obvious to others that you are fasting, but only to your Father, who is unseen; and your Father, who sees what is done in secret, will reward you.

Acts 14:23
Paul and Barnabas appointed elders for them in each church and, with prayer and fasting, committed them to the Lord, in whom they had put their trust.

Willpower. Want Power. God's Power

1 Thessalonians 5:16-18

[16]Rejoice always, [17]pray continually, [18]give thanks in all circumstances; for this is God's will for you in Christ Jesus.

Appendix C: Recommended Readings

Caputo, Michael. *Fasting: Eight Reasons Why Fasting Should Become a Part of Your Life*. Nashville: Thomas Nelson, 1982.

Feola, Kristen. *The Ultimate Guide to the Daniel Fast*. Grand Rapids: Zondervan, 2010.

Franklin, Jentezen. *The Fasting Edge: Recover Your Passion, Recapture Your Dream, Restore Your Joy*. Lake Mary: Charisma House, 2011.

Meyers, Joyce. *Look Great, Feel Great: 12 Keys to Enjoying a Healthy Life Now*. New York: Warner Faith, 2006.

Moss, Michael. *Salt, Sugar, Fat: How the Food Giants Hooked Us*. New York: Random House, 2013.

Pollan, Michael. *In Defense of Food*. New York: Penguin Books, 2008.

Richardson, Donna. *Witness to Fitness: Pumped Up! Powered Up! All Things Are Possible!* New York: HarperOne, 2012.

Shirer, Priscilla. *Breathe: Making Room for Sabbath*. Nashville: LifeWay Christian Resources, 2014.

Terry, Bryant. *Afro-Vegan: Farm-Fresh African, Caribbean, and Southern Flavors Remixed*. New York: Ten Speed Press, 2014.

Warren, Rick, Daniel Amen, & Mary Hyman. *The Daniel Plan: 40 Days to a Healthier Life*. Grand Rapids: Zondervan, 2013.

If you were helped by this book,
please share your thoughts and testimony.

Email nettye at book@nettyejohnson.com
or post on social media (Twitter or Instagram)
to @nettyejohnson with the hashtag
#TempleCare.

More from the Author

NEED A SPEAKER TO engage, educate, and inspire your group? Bring Nettye Johnson to your next event.

Nettye's presentations and workshops are an artful combination of research, experience, introspection, and practical application that touch and transform.

With a fun and interactive style, Nettye helps the audience see themselves in the subject, breaking complex issues into understandable solutions.

A former technical trainer, Nettye developed a passion for health education during her 10-year tenure with the nation's leading weight loss company. Her work in training, business development and operations on local, state and national levels impacted thousands. In this work, she was struck by the decline of health and wellness in our nation and the important need for holistic education, motivation, and support to effectively address this trend.

Combining intensive study on nutrition, exercise physiology and psychology, behavior modification, and special population support with two decades of corporate training and Christian education experience, she founded Nettye Johnson Faith and Fitness Services LLC, (NJFFS), a Christian wellness organization providing a holistic approach to health and wholeness.

A sought-after speaker and presenter, Nettye customizes deliverable to meet the needs of your group.

Participants will laugh, learn and leave inspired and equipped to change. To learn more, visit Nettye at www.nettyejohnson.com

Notes

Introduction

[1] Obesity and Overweight, 2015.

[2] Chronic Disease Overview, 2015.

[3] Belluck, 2005.

[4] All three statistics come from "Fat in Church," http://www.foxnews.com/opinion/2012/06/03/obesity-epidemic-in-america-churches.html, January 4, 2013.

[5] National Weight Control Registry, http://nwcr.ws.

Diets Do Work

[6] "The U.S. Weight Loss Market: 2015 Status Report & Forecast," https://www.bharatbook.com/healthcare-market-research-reports-467678/healthcare-industry-healthcare-market-research-reports-healthcare-industry-analysis-healthcare-sector1.html, January 2015, accessed December 25, 2015.

[7] Rick Warren, *The Daniel Plan: 40 Days to a Healthier Life* (Grand Rapids: Zondervan, 2013), pp. 18–21

[8] Centers for Disease Control and Prevention, "Leading Causes of Death," http://www.cdc.gov/nchs/fastats/leading-causes-of-death.htm, last updated September 30, 2015, accessed May 1, 2015.

[9] Centers for Disease Control and Prevention, "Chronic Disease Overview," http://www.cdc.gov/chronicdisease/overview/, page last updated August 26, 2015, accessed December 1, 2015.

[10] Felicia Wade, MD, "BMI: Is This Scale Broken For Black Women?" BlackDoctor.org, accessed Dec 15, 2015, http://blackdoctor.org/451648/bmi-and-african-american-women/.

[11] Centers for Disease Control and Prevention, "Black or African-American Populations," http://www.cdc.gov/minorityhealth/populations/REMP/black.html #Disparities, accessed Dec 15, 2015.

[12] Wade, Felicia, MD, "BMI: Is This Scale Broken For Black Women?" BlackDoctor.org, http://blackdoctor.org/451648/bmi-and-african-american-women/, accessed December 15, 2015.

[13] Scott Roberts, "Body-Composition Assessment and Evaluation" in *ACE Lifestyle & Weight Management Coach Manual*, ed. Daniel J. Green (San Diego: American Council on Exercise, 2011), pp. 241–245.

[14] Ibid, p. 246.

[15] Ibid.

[16] Ibid., pp. 246–247.

[17] "Preventive Services Covered Under the Affordable Care Act," U.S. Department of Health and Human Services, http://www.hhs.gov/healthcare/facts-and-features/fact-sheets/preventive-services-covered-under-aca/#CoveredPreventiveServicesforAdults

[18] Health Coach Certification, American Council on Exercise.

The Science of Weight Loss

[19] Debra Wein, "Nutritional Programming," in *ACE Lifestyle & Weight Management Coach Manual* (San Diego: American Council on Exercise, 2011), pp. 323–324.

Weight Loss Begins in Your Mind: Get Rid of Those ANTs

[20] Daniel G. Amen, *Change Your Brain, Change Your Body: Use Your Brain to Get and Keep the Body You Have Always Wanted* (New York: Three Rivers Press, 2010), p. 20.

Foundations for Healthy Weight Maintenance

[21] MG Siegler, "Eric Schmidt: Every 2 Days We Create As Much Information As We Did Up To 2003," *TechCrunch*, http://techcrunch.com/2010/08/04/schmidt-data/, August 4, 2010

[22] "How to Study Your Bible," Grace to You, http://www.gty.org/resources/positions/p16/how-to-study-your-bible, accessed December 15, 2015.

[23] Robertson McQuilkin, *Understanding and Applying the Bible* (Chicago: Moody Press, 2009), p. 164.

[24] Mark Hyman, MD, *Avoid the Hidden Dangers of High Fructose Corn Syrup*, video, 3:07, April 6, 2015, http://health.clevelandclinic.org/2015/04/avoid-the-hidden-dangers-of-high-fructose-corn-syrup-video/

[25] "About High Fructose Corn Syrup," http://sweetsurprise.com/.

[26] Office of Disease Prevention and Health Promotion, *Scientific Report of the 2015 Dietary Guidelines Advisory Committee*, http://health.gov/dietaryguidelines/2015-scientific-report/, last updated December 31, 2015.

[27] Mayo Clinic Staff, "Nutrition and Healthy Eating," http://www.mayoclinic.org/healthy-lifestyle/nutrition-and-healthy-eating/in-depth/meatless-meals/art-20048193.

[28] National Institutes of Health, "Risk in Red Meat?", http://www.nih.gov/news-events/nih-research-matters/risk-red-meat.

[29] Cleveland Clinic Heart & Vascular Team, "Researchers Find New Link Between Red Meat and Heart Disease," http://health.clevelandclinic.org/2014/11/researchers-find-new-link-between-red-meat-and-heart-disease-video/.

[30] Alexandra Sifferlan, "Grilled, Barbecued Meat Linked to Cancer Risk, Study Finds," *Time*, November 9, 2015, http://time.com/4104600/grilled-meat-barbecue-mutagens-cancer/.

[31] Physicians Committee for Responsible Medicine, "Meat Consumption and Cancer Risk," http://www.pcrm.org/health/cancer-resources/diet-cancer/facts/meat-consumption-and-cancer-risk.

[32] Anahad O'Conner, "Meat Is Linked to Higher Cancer Risk, W.H.O. Report Finds," *The New York Times*, October 27, 2015, http://www.nytimes.com/2015/10/27/health/report-links-some-types-of-cancer-with-processed-or-red-meat.html.

[33] Randy Molla, "How Much Meat Do Americans Eat? Then and Now," *The Wall Street Journal*, October 2, 2014, http://blogs.wsj.com/numbers/how-much-meat-do-americans-eat-then-and-now-1792/.

[34] David Pimentel and Marcia H. Pimentel, *Food, Energy, and Society*, 3rd ed. (Boca Raton: CRC Press, 2007), pp. 67–75.

[35] C. David Coats, *Old MacDonald's Factory Farm: The Myth of the Traditional Farm and the Shocking Truth about Animal Suffering in Today's Agribusiness* (New York: Crossroad Publishing Company, 1991), p. 13.

[36] John W. Ayers, Benjamin M. Althouse, Morgan Johnson, Mark Dredze, and Joanna E. Cohen, "What's the Healthiest Day? Circaseptan (Weekly) Rhythms in Healthy Considerations," *American Journal of Preventive Medicine* 47, no. 1 (2014): 73–76.

[37] Jane Black, "Meat on the Side: Modern Menus Shift the Focus to Vegetables," *The Wall Street Journal*, October 31, 2014, http://www.wsj.com/articles/meat-on-the-side-modern-menus-shift-the-focus-to-vegetables-1414784266, accessed December 12, 2015.

[38] Mayo Clinic Staff, "Nutrition and Healthy Eating," http://www.mayoclinic.org/healthy-lifestyle/nutrition-and-healthy-eating/in-depth/meatless-meals/art-20048193.

[39] Kathleen Zelman, "With Fruits and Veggies, More Matters," http://www.webmd.com/food-recipes/fruits-veggies-more-matters.

[40] United States Department of Agriculture, Agricultural Research Service, National Nutrient Database for Standard Reference Release 28, http://ndb.nal.usda.gov/.

[41] This section is based on the following sources: www.sugarscience.org; Alice G. Walton, "How Much Sugar Are Americans Eating? [Infographic]," August 30, 2012, http://www.forbes.com/sites/alicegwalton/2012/08/30/how-much-sugar-are-americans-eating-infographic/; Carolyn Gregoire, "This Is What Sugar Does to Your Brain," *The Huffington Post*, April 6, 2015, http://www.huffingtonpost.com/2015/04/06/sugar-brain-mental-health_n_6904778.html; William Dufty, "Refined Sugar – The Sweetest Poison of All ...," Global Healing Center, http://www.globalhealingcenter.com/sugar-problem/refined-sugar-the-sweetest-poison-of-all; American Heart Association, "Added Sugars," http://www.heart.org/HEARTORG/GettingHealthy/NutritionCenter/HealthyEating/Added-Sugars_UCM_305858_Article.jsp#.VoVrEEo4GM9

[42] Carolyn Gregoire, "This Is What Sugar Does to Your Brain," *The Huffington Post*, April 6, 2015, http://www.huffingtonpost.com/2015/04/06/sugar-brain-mental-health_n_6904778.html

[43] Mark Hyman, MD, "Stopping Addiction to Sugar: Willpower or Genetics?" last updated October 18, 2014, http://drhyman.com/blog/2011/02/04/stopping-addiction-to-sugar-willpower-or-genetics/.

[44] American Heart Association, "Added Sugars," http://www.heart.org/HEARTORG/GettingHealthy/NutritionCente r/HealthyEating/Added-Sugars_UCM_305858_Article.jsp#.VoVrEE04GM9

[45] http://www.SugarScience.org.

[46] The White House, "First Lady Michelle Obama to Ask Everyone to "Drink Up" with More Water," September 12, 2013, https://www.whitehouse.gov/the-press-office/2013/09/12/first-lady-michelle-obama-ask-everyone-drink-more-water, accessed December 17, 2015.

[47] Nina K., "Can You Lose Body Fat by Stopping Drinking Soda?" *SFGate.com*, http://healthyeating.sfgate.com/can-lose-body-fat-stopping-drinking-soda-7728.html, accessed December 17, 2015.

[48] Stephen Sinatra, "Is Your Sleep Schedule Setting You Up for a Heart Attack or Stroke?" http://www.drsinatra.com/is-your-sleep-schedule-setting-you-up-for-a-heart-attack-or-stroke/, last reviewed December 16, 2015, accessed February 14, 2014.

[49] Anne Harding, "How Lack of Sleep Hurts Your Health," Health.com, http://www.health.com/health/condition-article/0,,20573185,00.html, last updated February 23, 2012, accessed December 17, 2015.

[50] National Sleep Foundation, "Healthy Sleep Tips," https://sleepfoundation.org/sleep-tools-tips/healthy-sleep-tips, accessed February 12, 2014.

Adopt a Food Philosophy

[51] Michael Pollan, *In Defense of Food: An Eater's Manifesto* (New York: The Penguin Group, 2008), front matter.

[52] Michael Moss, *Salt, Sugar, Fat: How the Food Giants Hooked Us* (New York: Random House, 2013), p. xvii.

[53] Ted Winn, "Balance," Song, Shanachie, 2009.

[54] Abraham Joshua Heschel, *The Sabbath* (New York: Farrar Straus Giroux, 2005), pp. 22–23.

[55] Judith Beck, *The Beck Diet Solution: Train Your Brain to Think Like a Thin Person* (Birmingham: Oxmoor House, 2009).

Experience Food

[56] Institute for Quality and Efficiency in Health Care, "How Does Our Sense of Taste Work?" PubMed Health, http://www.ncbi.nlm.nih.gov/pubmedhealth/PMH0072592/, last updated January 6, 2012, accessed December 17, 2015.

[57] Josh Bishop, "Digesting Grace: Why the Food We Eat Matters to God," *Christianity Today*, August 15, 2012, http://www.christianitytoday.com/thisisourcity/7thcity/digesting-grace.html, accessed December 20, 2015.

Explore Food

[58] Bryant Terry, *Afro-Vegan: Farm-Fresh African, Caribbean and Southern Flavors Remixed* (Berkeley: Ten Speed Press, 2014), p. 2.

Embrace the Fast

[59] *Asceticism* comes from the Greek word *askēsis*, which means training, or bodily exercise. Asceticism is defined as rigorous self-denial for spiritual purposes.

[60] Jentezen Franklin, *The Fasting Edge: Recover Your Passion, Reclaim Your Purpose, Restore Your Joy* (Lake Mary: Charisma Media, 2011), p. 206.

Willpower. Want Power. God's Power

[61] American Psychological Association, "Stress a Major Health Problem in the U.S., Warns APA," October 24, 2007, http://www.apa.org/news/press/releases/2007/10/stress.aspx, accessed December 19,2015.

[62] Ephesians 3:20-21 KJV